HINDUISM FOR THE NEXT GENERATION

HINDUISM
FOR THE
NEXT
GENERATION

V. KRISHNAMURTHY

Former Professor of Mathematics & Dy. Director,
Birla Institute of Technology & Science,
PILANI (INDIA)

25

PUBLISHING
FOR ONE WORLD
WILEY EASTERN LIMITED
New Delhi • Bangalore • Bombay • Calcutta • Guwahati
Hyderabad • Lucknow • Madras • Pune

WILEY EASTERN LIMITED
4835/24, Ansari Road, Daryaganj, New Delhi 110 002
27, Bull Temple Road, Basavangudi, Bangalore 560 004
P. Box No. 4124, Saraswati Mandir School, Nana Chowk,
    Kennedy Bridge, Bombay 400 007
40/8, Ballygunge Circular Road, Calcutta 700 019
Pan Bazar, Rani Bari, Guwahati 781 001
1-2-412/9, Gaganmahal near A.V. College, Damalguda, Hyderabad 500 029
13, Pandit Madan Mohan Malviya Marg, Lucknow 226 001
No. 6, Ist Main Road, Gandhi Nagar, Madras 600 020
Indira Co-operative Housing Society Ltd. (Indira Height)
    Flat No. 2, Building No. 7, Erandwane, Paud Fatta, Pune 411 038

ISBN 81-224-0382-4

Published by V.S. Johri for Wiley Eastern Limited,
4835/24, Ansari Road, Daryaganj, New Delhi 110 002,
Composed by Phoenix Computer Centre, Delhi-95 and
printed by Taj Press, Bahadurgarh Road, Delhi 110 006
PRINTED IN INDIA

Dedicated to
My
Father
SRI R. VISVANATHA SASTRIGAL
(1882–1956)

Preface

Hinduism is a complex religion not easily intelligible to even the insiders, if they isolate themselves from a Hindu environment. In particular, those who live outside India, feel the responsibility of having themselves to transmit the culture, religion and philosophy of Hinduism to their next generation. This burden was not felt by them when they were in India because the environment took care of it, though only partly or tangentially. Any one who has talked to Hindu families in the world outside India, would have discovered the intense anguish in the minds of such parents to somehow be able to tell their sons and daughters about Hinduism, its richness, its glory, its achievements, its philosophy and its liberal mindedness both in terms of divisions within and in terms of religions outside of it. In the course of such interactions by the author, with friends and families in the USA, a few lectures came to be delivered during the months of September, October, 1989 on certain aspects of Hinduism—in particular, on matters associated with religious worship. This book is an outcome of those lectures. Naturally it has turned out to be a detailed discussion of the widespread concern for what should be held as the minimum expectations from the Hindu of the future in the modern fast life. In fact at one time a title that was considered for the book was: WHAT EVERY NON-RESIDENT INDIAN HINDU PARENT SHOULD KNOW ABOUT RELIGIOUS WORSHIP.

It is suggested that the chapters be read in sequence. Though many of the ideas occur repeatedly, as one proceeds through the sequence of the chapters, each time the idea recurs it is taken up at a further depth and detail. All mythological Samskrit names and technical Samskrit words—except the most-often occurring ones: Rama, Krishna, Arjuna, Karma, Yoga, Gita and Avatar—are italicised and explained the first time they occur.

Each of the lectures given was followed by a question-answer session and the brief answers that were given at the time have been elaborated in a separate chapter entitled: Questions and Answers: Problems and Solutions.

The author would like to record his grateful thanks to (i) the following organizations/institutions where the lectures were delivered:

Round Rock High School, Round Rock, Texas;

Seminar in the Community Church of Cedar Hills, Portland, Oregon;

Faith Presbyterian Church, Austin, Texas;

Fine Arts Association of Arizona, Tempe, Arizona;

ASU India Student Association, Tempe, Arizoha;

Hindu Temple Association of Delaware, Wilmington, Delaware

Several Associations of Indian families at Austin, Texas and at Boston, Massachusettes, and (ii) to the following individuals who were instrumental in the arrangement of the lectures:

Dr. S. Umapathy, Andover, MA

Dr. Ranganathan, Andover, MA

Dr. Arjun C. Sau, Wilmington, DE

Dr. N.S. Subramanian, Wilmington, DE

Dr. K. Raghunathan, Austin, TX

Dr. Sridhar, Austin, TX

Mrs. Usha Krishnamurthy, Austin, TX

Mr. Keith Wright, Austin, TX.

Dr. Satish Goela, Round Rock, TX

Dr. K. Balasubramanian, Chandler, AZ

Dr. A.K. Narasimhan, Mesa, AZ

Mrs. Priya Krishnamurthy, Aloha, OR

Mr. Irv Lamon, Beaverton, OR

Mrs. Susan Tetrick, Beaverton, OR

'Kamalalaya', 4, Papani Apts.   V. Krishnamurthy
6, 67th Street, Ashoknagar,
Madras 600 083, India.

Contents

Page

Preface

1. Hinduism: A Simple Overview   1

2. Hindu Religious Worship: A Classroom Lesson   9
   for the Novice

3. Bhakti in Hinduism: An Advanced Lesson for
   the Faithful   20

4. Krishnavatara, the Miraculous   32

5. Hinduism—Attitudes, not Rituals   44

6. What it is to Live as a Hindu?   58

7. Questions and Answers; Problems and Solutions   73

CHAPTER 1

Hinduism: A Simple Overview

Hinduism is an ancient religion and one of the major religions of the world. To take up the task of presenting it in a single essay is a formidable task. So we shall highlight only the bare essentials and that too, without any sophistication. The first distinguishing feature that anybody notes about Hinduism is that it has no founder who started the religion. Also there is no single event or sequence of events which may be cited as responsible for the founding, if any, of the religion. In this sense, it differs from almost all other religions of the world.

According to the *Vedas* which are the supreme authority for everything in Hinduism, there is only one God. You may call Him by any name and give Him any form. The wise call Him by several names. He is present everywhere and at all times. This unique Godhead, this Divinity, is in everything that we see, hear, smell, touch or feel. He is in every inanimate object and He is in every animate being. He is in our heart of hearts. But then why don't we see Him or feel His presence? It is because our minds are so impure. If we can get rid of all the impurities from the innermost recesses of our hearts, Hinduism asserts, we can certainly see Him, reflected in the crystalline purity of our heart and mind.

To be able to see it and live in the constant awareness of the presence of that Divinity is the purpose of life. In that living presence of the reflection of God in our mind, we must be tuned to the frequency of that Divinity and be of service to society— this is what we are for.

Anything that we do which encourages or is concordant with the above process of realisation of God's presence in us is called *Punya* or Merit. Anything that we do or think that takes us away from that realisation is called *papa* (the samskrit word for sin). Truth, non-violence, humility, compassion, sympathy, unselfish service to society, helping the poor, the depressed and the sick —these are certainly among the well-known *Punyas* of Hinduism, as in any other religion. If one accumulates a large amount of extraordinary *Punya* to his credit he goes to heaven after death, to enjoy, for a specified period of time, the fruits of his *Punya*. If one accumulates a large amount of extreme sin he goes to Hell, to suffer the punishment for all that sin, again for a specified period. But the large majority of humanity do not belong to either category and are only a mixture of ordinary *Punyas* and ordinary sins. This large majority of people are born again in this world. This last one is the second most distinguishing feature of Hinduism.

Everyone who is born has to die some time or other. But when the body dies the soul does not die. The soul is born again in another body. The mind also goes along with the soul, though it does not remember what it did in the previous body. The mind and soul, together individualized in this fashion, go on from body to body again and again. This is the unique principle of transmigration. When the soul travels like this from body to body, carrying along with it the mind which has in some sense, irrevocably, attached itself to it, the mind on its own, carries a heavy luggage within itself, namely, all the impurities which it has collected in each of its sojourns in a body. The mind is like the wind which carries the smell of a rose garden through which it has blown, even long after it has left the garden. Like the wind which has passed through a filthy and stinking place, the mind carries the stink which it has collected in its previous births and lives into its succeeding births. The soul knows no good or bad, but the mind which is with it carries all the good and bad imprints in it, which reflect themselves as the tendencies of the person in his present birth. A mind which has in its previous births helped the poor, has been sympathetic, compassionate and noble carries such tendencies in its future lives. This is why we see some people from their very birth are very noble and gentle and some people, if we may say so, stink!. Thus are born the tendencies and in-born nature of people. These tendencies are known technically as *Vasanas*. *Vasana* means smell. So the smell of purity or the smell of impurity which one carries from one's actions in one's previous lives is what distinguishes person from person even though each has the same pure Divinity in oneself. This cycle of transmigration of soul and mind will end only when man realises the presence of Divinity in himself and 'reaches' God. This will happen when his inner mind is devoid of all imprints of any kind whatsoever, in other words, devoid of all *vasanas*. This is the state of Salvation of Man. Thereafter he never has to be born again. Even souls which go to Heaven or Hell because of an extreme *Punya* or extraordinary sin, have to come back to be born as human beings on earth in order to continue on their path of evolution. The ultimate destination of all souls is to merge in the Supreme Presence of God.

God is the only Reality which is ever present, in
the past, in the present and in the future. Anything else
is transient. The only Truth is God and He has no name
or form. He is therefore an Impersonal Absolute, though
we have used the pronoun He here. Anything that we
see is His creation. When we think of Him as the
Creator, we call Him *Brahma*. Anything that is created
has to be dissolved. When God takes up this function
of Dissolution or Destruction we call Him *Siva*. When
we think of Him as our Protector and the Saviour we
call Him *Vishnu*. The same unique Godhead of Hinduism has these three major functions. The three Gods
of these functions form a Trinity. But actually there is
only one God which we speak of as three. Whether we
worship *Brahma, Vishnu* or *Siva*, we are worshipping the
same Absolute Godhead.

Since God is present in all beings and in all creation of His, He is present in all Nature. Every inanimate object is also a manifestation of His presence. So
we can worship Him in any form whatsoever. This is
the basis of idol worship in Hinduism and this is the
third most distinguishing feature of Hinduism. God is
worshipped through images, or idols or pictures of Him
as imagined by us. Usually a newcomer to Hinduism
is confused about this idol worship. An idol is like the
flag for an army. The flag is not the country but it definitely stands for the country and one is prepared to die
for it. So also an idol is a symbol of God. In fact, any
symbol is good enough. The mind cannot worship in
abstraction. So Hinduism says: Worship God in any
form you like, the form is not important; the name is
not to be debated; it is the intensity of devotion to God
that matters. It is the attitude of worship, called Bhakti,
in Samskrit, that is of real consequence. Any one of the

three Gods of the Trinity can be worshipped in this way and each such worship will purify the mind, which is the objective of all worship. Worshipping an idol in the tradition of Hinduism does not mean we are worshipping that inanimate object as God in a pagan way, but it means that we are worshipping that omnipresent Divinity in the form of the idol before us. We are worshipping God in the idol and not the idol as God.

There is another distinguishing feature of Hinduism which is present in no other religion. Just as the three Gods of the Trinity, namely, *Brahma*, *Vishnu* and *Siva* are only the same unique Godhead manifested in different functions and forms so also there are other manifestations of God in the mythological history of India. God's Will is supreme. So whenever He wants He can appear in this world as a concrete person or being in flesh and blood. This he has done many times. In fact, every time there has been a decline of natural order in the Universe, every time there has been a rise of cruelty and evil, God has manifested Himself. Each such appearance is called an Avatar. (Avatar means descent). The Impersonal Absolute Godhead, descends, as it were, to the level of our ordinary concrete universe and makes its presence felt in flesh and blood. The Perfect God takes on, it seems, an imperfection in itself to appear as a living being in order to take us, imperfect beings, on the onward path to Perfection.! So whenever such an event takes place, as when the Son of God appeared on Earth, the people of that time who have the beatific experience of God's proximate presence, consider themselves very fortunate and worship Him as God. And this is how, every Avatar, in Hinduism, has come to be worshipped as God. These Avatars are the closest approximations to Divinity for us, who cannot see Him in ourselves.

Once He appeared as Man-Lion, (*Nara-simha*, in Samskrit, meaning half-man, half-lion), in order to put an end to the extreme cruelty which a very powerful but inhuman king was perpetrating on the world. Actually the son of this King was very devoted to Lord *Vishnu* but the King in his arrogance wanted himself to be recognised as the only God, the God, of this universe. After many futile attempts to convert his son to his viewpoint, the King asked his son to show him this God Vishnu whom he was worshipping. In extreme anger, he showed a pillar and asked: Is your God in this pillar? The son, *Prahlada*, with supreme confidence in the omnipresence of the Lord, said, YES. And lo and behold, God obliged His devotee by appearing in the form of a Man-Lion from that pillar. This Man-Lion proved to be the end of the King. The fact that He appeared as a Man-Lion itself has a history behind it. In short, it was because the King, by his own supernatural prowess was under a spell that he could never be killed by any human being or by any being of the animal kingdom. This Man-Lion Avatar of God, which occurred for a very specific purpose, is one of the earliest Avatars of Vishnu in the mythology of India. It shows the efficacy of a full-fledged faith in the omnipresence of God. Prahlada is the model of such faith.

There are two most famous Avatars of God— without a knowledge of which, even a summary presentation of Hinduism is not complete. These are Rama and Krishna, the two names with which the entire Hindu India will reverberate wherever you go. Millions of years ago, there lived a King *Ravana* by name who was destroying all the good things that the *Rishis* were doing to propitiate God and for the good of humanity. His powers were so great that no ordinary divine power could match him. Finally Lord *Vishnu* by His own Will, was born as the son in a royal family. This son of God was known as Rama. The word Rama means, in Samskrit, the Ultimate Reality of everything. Rama and His consort *Sita* by various circumstances underwent many sufferings by living fourteen years in the forest, away from civilisation and away from luxury and comfort. Finally Rama had to fight all the evil men who worked for *Ravana* and in the end *Ravana* himself was destroyed with all his clan. This manifestation of God as Rama is a central thread in the vast fabric of Hinduism, just as Resurrection is the central kingpin of Christianity. Rama and Jesus had many things in common. Both were a great colossus of humility without the least shade of arrogance. Both undertook suffering on themselves for the rest of humanity. Jesus died on the Cross so that humanity may be saved for God. Rama lived a life of truth, compassion and virtue throughout his long life and showed to the world how we must not only be prepared to sacrifice but in reality renounce every single attachment of ourselves, for the happiness of the rest of the world.

The Avatar of Krishna happened five thousand years ago in the city of Mathura in North India. Again it was the same reason: Protection of the virtuous and the destruction of the wicked. Krishna's story has several parallels with the life of Jesus. The birth itself was a miracle. And in his life he performed several miracles. Once he had to carry a whole hill on his shoulders in order to protect the entire community from destruction through Nature's fury. Krishna's life is in another sense most important for Hinduism because He condensed all the truths and philosophy of Hinduism in 700 simple verses and taught it directly to one of the most well-known characters in the history of Hinduism, namely, Arjuna. This teaching is called the *Bhagavad-Gita*, the Song of the Lord or the Divine Song or Poem. In fact for those who cannot go back to the entire *Vedas* to understand Hinduism, the Gita has everything in it. It is very much relevant even in the modern context. The final teaching of the Gita is: Do your work in an unselfish way. Even if your duty leads you on to do apparently unjustifiable things, put the burden on God and do your duty. Do not keep on worrying about what is going to happen in the future. Have faith in the ultimate Divinity of every being. Love and serve every being. Each being has the same Divinity in them as what you have in you. If you serve God and humanity with humility and surrender to the Will of God you have nothing to fear either in this life or in the after-life. Do not be carried away by the transient ups and downs of every day life. And leave the problem of Salvation to God. He will take care of it.

The really most distinguishing feature of Hinduism is, however, that it is a matter of faith with the Hindus to consider all religions as true. Since God can be worshipped in several forms and several ways, Hindus consider different religions as so many paths to God. No religion should think that it is the only true religion. Each is a path to the same one God. And so there should be no hate or distrust of another religon or another point of view with respect to God. In this modern world of strife and hatred this tolerance of other religions and other points of view with respect to God is one of the major lessons that the world has to learn from the Hindu way of life. Even within Hinduism, you can choose that path which suits your taste, evolution, training and tradition. The only thing that is important is there should be no feeling of selfishness or egoism.

CHAPTER 2

Hindu Religious Worship:
A Classroom Lesson for the Novice

Hinduism is probably the most ancient religion alive today. We do not even know what it was known as in those ancient times. Actually we are talking about pre-historic times when we are talking about the origins of Hinduism. The one thing we know for certain is that what the Hindus consider as their most sacred liter-ature today, viz., the *Vedas* goes back to those times and has come down to us almost in the same form as it was then. This is one of the first mysteries that a student learns about Hinduism. The *Vedas*, collectively, consti-tute the scriptural authority for Hinduism. They are written in the Samskrit language. In fact they were never written down by anybody. They have come down from generation to generation by word of mouth. They are recited and studied in a characteristically unique way with specific intonations and accents so that there could be no interpolation or deletion of the text by anybody at any time. The text has been preserved in the same form for as long as, probably, five thousand years. The earliest time when they were p t to writing was the early nineteenth century when Western scholars brought out the printed version of the *Vedas* directly from the recitations given by the experts. There are actually four such *Vedas*. The smallest of them is about three to four times as big as the new testament. These *Vedas* form the oldest piece of recorded human expressions on Earth. They talk about God, about Nature, about man, morality, the Ultimate Reality of life, what happens after death, the fight that goes on in one's mental make-up between good and evil, rituals to propitiate gods of the heavens, man's duties to the gods of the cosmos and so on and, finally they contain long beautiful poems of praise of the Divine and several records of spiritual experiences by great thinkers called *Rishis* in ancient times. This last part is called the *Upanishads*, which are the most treasured philosophical treatises, discussions and discourses on fundamental matters of life and death, mind and soul, bondage and freedom, what is transient and ephemeral, what is permanent, what is the ultimate reality and what is the purpose of life. Throughout, the one message that the *Upanishads* are never tired of repeating is: Man is essentially divine.

During the period of the *Vedas* as well as in later periods of Hinduism, the one idea that has never been questioned is the transmigratory career of man's soul. In other words man's soul travels from body to body in its journey of evolution. The central core of the Hindu teaching is contained in this. Though man is basically divine, the divine is clothed in material external coverings and is camouflaged by the cloud of dirt accumulated by the mind. Mind clings to the soul in a subtle way throughout its transmigratory career. Mind is a nebulous thing which keeps on accumulating impressions, memories and habits of thinking. These constitute the *Vasanas* of the mind or of the person to whom it clings for the moment.

Vasana means smell. These *Vasanas* are the ones which give the individual his mental personality even before his upbringing in this life starts having an effect on him. It is something over which you have no control, because it belongs to your past. This past determines your level of evolution as of now and also your tendencies for human behavior. If they are bad, you have to contend with them and fight them. This is the meaning of Karma theory. As far as the future is concerned you are totally free to create new *vasanas* for yourself. But if you are going to be carried away by the already existing *vasanas* in your system, and they happen to carry you into undesirable avenues, it is nobody's fault except yourself. In this sense you are the architect of your fate. But in the sense that your tendencies are born with you and you have had no control with them when you were born, to that extent you are ruled by your fate.

In man's journey to perfection, the ultimate aim is to shed off all these *vasanas* of the mind, so that the mind, in its pristine, unloaded, crystalline purity may reflect the presence of Divinity, which the *Vedas* assure us, is there in every one of us. For this upward path towards perfection, in addition to emphasizing certain basic virtues like purity, humility, self-control and truth, like all other religions, Hinduism emphasizes two more, namely, non-violence and detachment. Non-violence stems from the fact that everything is but a spark of the same divinity and therefore no harm should be done to anything that is living. Detachment is non-attachment to anything which is not ultimately permanent. What is impermanent? Anything that is amenable to sense perception is impermanent. What is not amenable to sense perception? The Ultimate Reality is the one that is not amenable to sense perception. This is the common substratum of existence both in the microcosmic and in the macrocosmic universe. In other words, our body, our senses, our mind, our intellect, our possessions, our kith and kin—none of these is ultimate.

This Ultimate Substratum is in fact the essence of everything that is amenable to sense perception. This Reality is the supreme Godhead of Hinduism. There is no other, no second. It is formless, nameless and totally unaffected by anything. It just is. *Brahman* is the name given to this and the naming itself is a slip of rigour though intended. *Brahman* comes from the word 'to transcend' and so it connotes that which transcends everything that we know. But the moment we think of it as a God to be worshipped, we have already brought, by our limited intellect, a subject-object relationship in respect of the ultimate Godhead which has no second. We have actually violated the uniqueness of *Brahman*, the moment we even think of it. If we are to cite a parallel to it in our every day experience, the only thing we may refer to is modern physics. The moment we observe a subatomic particle, what we observe has already been influenced by our observation. These rules of modern physics may not apply to *Brahman*. But our very definition of *Brahman* says that you cannot predicate anything of it except that it is. You cannot say that it is large or small, black or white, you cannot point it out and say it is this or that, you cannot possess it, you cannot relate to it. The *Upanishads* get out of this bottleneck by postulating what they call a *Saguna Brahman*, meaning, *Brahman* with attributes. This is nothing but the Ultimate reality looked at from our world of experience. The other name for this is *Iswara*. This is the Almighty that corresponds to the unique God of other religions.

This Almighty is the God whom we can think of, worship, invoke, revere, relate to, pray to and in this sense the ultimate God of the Hindus. This has all the superhuman and superlative qualities that we can think of—with infinite mercy, with infinite compassion, with infinite grace and infinite potentialities.

But here comes a subtle point. According to the scriptures, God is both transcendent and immanent, omniscient, omnipotent and omnipresent and therefore by giving it any single name or form we are delimiting its omnipresence and transcendence. No name or form therefore will exclusively describe it and by that very reason, say the *Vedas*, all names and forms suit it. This is the thin end of the wedge. In other words, the totality of things that are perceptible in the universe is permeated by God. Everything is divine. Divinity is inherent in everything that we see, smell, hear, touch or feel. In fact it is in every one of us. If we are not able to see it, it is because we are governed by our sense perception. We have to transcend space and time and cease to be ourselves in order to realise its presence.

Since the common mind of man cannot comprehend this abstractness and transcendence of the nameless and formless version of God, different idols and images enter the picture. Each one has a mythology behind it or a philosophical or esoteric interpretation as its undercurrent. These myriad symbols, images and idols are only symbols, images and idols and they are not substitutes for God. This every thinking Hindu knows though he may not know the exact mythological context or esoteric meaning which that idol, image or symbol carries. Each one indicates the Supreme Power inherent in every body and it is that One God which is worshipped in the form of idols and images.

These images may be just stones or trees or other inanimate objects or they may be anthropomorphic repli-
cas of a certain manifestation of that Supreme Divinity.
In the course of the mythological history of India—
which is actually the prehistoric period—several such
manifestations of that one Godhead has taken place,
sometimes for the purpose of putting an end to the col-
losal wickedness of a demon or sometimes for the purpose of showering divine grace on a superhuman
devotee of that divinity. If any one thinks that these different gods and goddesses are something like the Greek
gods and goddesses and they are warring for supremacy among themselves, one is totally mistaken. The
principle that there is only one Godhead and that Godhead is nameless and formless and for that very reason
all names and forms suit it is stated in the *Vedas* itself
and repeated many times throughout the vast scriptural
literature. This fundamental point is the most important lesson that one should learn about Hinduism
whether he grows within the environment or out of it.
It is difficult to miss this lesson if one lives in India even
for a short time and observes with a discerning intellect. An idol serves the same purpose for a religious
devotee as a flag does for an army. Any worship for
that matter introduces a duality between the worship-
per and the worshipped and so is a comedown from
the unique mental cognition of the Divinity inherent in
oneself. Hinduism is human enough to admit within
its fold even those ordinary mortals who cannot rise,
in their understanding, above the grossly concrete rep-
resentations of God. Hinduism says, in essence, each
individual can worship God in whatever form that suits
his competence, taste, and stage of spiritual evolution.
    There are certainly several rituals for worship. But

these rituals vary in detail from region to region, from tradition to tradition and from time to time. This variety is because of the in-built flexibilities in the practice of Hinduism and because of the largeness of the subcontinent with different roots in culture. But always the technique of worship is to invoke the god of worship in some kind of a picture or an idol or a lump of sandal paste or some specific types of stones mentioned for the purpose and then offer a *Puja* (= ritual worship) to it. This *Puja* consists of sixteen formalities like, invocation, offering a seat, offering water for various purposes, offering water, honey and milk for bath, offering cloth for dressing, offering flowers as obeisance and finally offering an eatable. The *Puja* always ends with an *arti*, which is a ceremonial waving of lighted comphor and last of all, prostrations, which indicate a total surrender to God. The very invocation, which is the first formality, contains the essence of the Hindu teaching, it says: Oh God! I know you are omnipresent. But, for the purpose of my concentration and worship please condescend to make your presence felt here in this idol (image, picture or stone or whatever) for the period of the puja; maybe I am insulting your omnipresence by requesting you to confine yourself to this form, but please pardon me; I know no other way. All this is contained in the *mantra* (vedic chant) that is used for the invocation. In every formality of the Puja the *mantra* that is recited carries such high philosophical thinking within itself.

In all these formalities, it is the attitude that matters rather than the real thing you offer. You may just offer some flowers and say that instead of the silken dress you would like to offer the Lord, you are offering these flowers. Similarly instead of pouring water

over the image or the picture for bath you may just
sprinkle water on it and say this may be taken as bath.
The five elements being the ultimate purifier of all
things in the universe, Hindu tradition uses them effec-
tively for such purposes in all their rituals. It is mostly
either water or fire. So every time something has to be
purified, the relevant quotation from scriptures is
recited and water sprinkled on the deity before you. In
temples where the images of gods have been built in
stone or metal for this very purpose,the daily *puja* will
have elaborate procedures for ritually and physically
bathing the idol and this is called *Abhisheka*. A *Puja* at
home may take as small a time as five minutes or as
long a time as four to six hours. The eatable that you
finally offer to the deity is technically called *Naivedya*—
the word simply meaning, that which is shown to God.
It could be any sweet dish, fruits, coconuts or any other
specially prepared dish and after thus being offered to
God—which the deity does not eat, of course—is then
shared by those who have attended the *Puja* and their
friends and well-wishers. In fact Hindu scriptures are
very clear that nothing should be eaten without first
being formally offered to God, and therefore nothing
should be eaten which are not offerable to God. Flowers are one offering to God which we do not take back
in full. Flowers come from nature, that is *Prakriti* and
go back to the Lord of that *Prakriti*, namely, God. Since
flowers are the only thing which we can wholly leave
with the deity of worship, Hindu deity worship always
emphasizes a massive use of flowers. Even the water
which is used for bathing the deity is taken back in little
drops as lustral water, in the hollow of the right hand
and swallowed immediately. When anything is offered
to God and then taken back for our use like this,

it becomes *Prasad*, meaning Grace (of God). This takes us to the next topic: Bhakti and Grace.

Bhakti means devotion, but it actually connotes an attitude of intense devotion. In practice it gets exhibited in several ways. One of the most common and most recommended by the scriptures is that of reciting God's names. There are several purposes in such a recitation: to purify oneself; to give expression to one's Bhakti; to progress on the upward path of evolution; to obtain God's Grace for a specific material purpose; to obtain God's Grace and through that ultimate Salvation. For such purposes of recitation of God's names and glories there are innumerable poems of praise (*stotras*) in the secondary scriptural literature. The *Vedas* are the primary scriptures. All the others like the *Ramayana*, written by *Valmiki*, the *Mahabharata*, written by *Vyasa* and the 36 *Puranas* and their associates all written by *Vyasa* are among the secondary scriptures. These poems of praise and their recitations constitute one more of the distinguishing features of Hinduism and can be recognised to be the one vibrant chord that runs through the cultural milieu of Hindu India throughout the length and breadth of the country. Particularly after the bleak middle ages when Hinduism had to undergo several shocks from the intolerance of some of the invaders it had to face, there was a renaissance. This is the period generally from the 10th century to the 18th century when a large number of intense devotees of God appeared on the scene in different parts of India. They preached and practised the *Nama Sankirtana* (= reciting of God's names) method of obtaining God's Grace, in preference to the much misused ritualistic tradition handed down by the Vedic age. The enormous amount of devotional literature that exists in India, both in

Samskrit and in Tamil—which are the two most ancient languages—, but also in the other major languages of the country, has been inspired by hundreds of saints, musicians, mystics and great poets all over India, almost without a break through this period.

Some of these poems of praise in the scriptural literature are litanies of one hundred or one thousand names of God. These are full of flowering poetry, alliteration, rhythm and rich philosophical content. The names listed are those of God, extolling His majesty and splendour, omnipresence and omniscience, transcendence and immanence and His exploits in His different manifestations. To repeat these is to enjoy the ecstasy of divine communion. In addition to these recitations, for those who are not educated in these, there are innumerable *bhajans*—streamlined repetitions of God's names,which can be sung in chorus to set beats. These again were popularised by those great devotees of the renaissance period. The very popular *Hare Rama bhajan* sung by those involved in the Krishna Consciousness group is an example of this tradition. These *bhajans* and recitations are intended to tune you to the frequency of the divine in you and rouse your divine instinct. The fundamental belief of Hinduism being the divinity of man, the divine instincts that are latent in oneself are touched by these bhajans and recitations and in due time will conquer the baser instincts which are themselves only the consequences of one's *vasanas* acquired in this and all previous lives.

The obtaining of God's Grace is the much-sought after goal of Bhakti. There are two views in Hinduism regarding the methodology for obtaining Grace of God. One view, which is called the monkey theory says that the devotee has to make enough efforts by himself for

God to descend to him, just as the baby monkey has to cling to its mother of its own for being carried along. On the other hand, the other viewpoint, which is called the cat theory, says that the devotee does not have to make any effort because God Himself will take care of him and do the needful. This is like the Presbyterian viewpoint in Christianity. The cat theory implies a total surrender. The weight of scriptural authority leans towards this theory. This is in fact a surrender wherein the devotee surrenders even his mind to the Lord. He has no mind of his own thereafter. One is reminded of a nineteenth century Christian hymn: Oh Lord, take my will and make it thine; it shall no longer be mine; take my heart, it is thine own; it shall be thy royal throne. This is the Bhakti Yoga of Hinduism.

CHAPTER 3

Bhakti in Hinduism:
An Advanced Lesson for the Faithful

Bhakti means intense devotion. The concept of devotion is more or less the same in all religions. But in Hinduism there are certain extra subtleties which make the subject comparatively more complicated. These are three in number: viz., (a) the One Reality versus many Gods of worship, (b) Idol worship and freedom to choose an *Ishta Devata* and (c) the interactive ramifications of God's Grace, Fate and Free Will. An integrated but brief presentation of all these will be attempted here in the context of Bhakti.

Morality and ethics are only the first steps in the religious life of a man. Man's mental anguish very often takes him to situations wherein he needs the solace of a more superior power than himself. In his first stages of such introspection he ends up discovering the superiority of Nature over him. This makes him analyse the powers of Nature and then he discovers that however deep he penetrates into the complexity of nature there is something deeper than what he knows. This is actually the progress of his scientific spirit. But man actually took several centuries of his civilised life to arrive

at this stage. Long before he arrived at this stage he had
already postulated a Supreme Cosmic Power as the
motive force behind every expression of Nature. In the
early history of Man's ascent this perhaps gave him the
motivation to invent the concept of God. But the concept of God in Hinduism is more complex than this
naive conception of a Cosmic Power. The *Upanishads*
take pains to explain how every physical expression
amenable to sense perception is nothing but an expression of the divine. Since everything is God, you should
not delineate it by one name and form and circumscribe
it by the limitations of worldly expressions and imag-
ery. In fact, anything that has name and form is a creation of the human mid. So we have to transcend the
concept of name and form to get to the true nature of
God. The *Upanishads* declare that there is a substratum
of existence behind all the mainifest presentations to
the mind. This is just like gold being the substratum
of existence in all gold ornaments, plastic being the substratum of existence in all articles of plastic or the movie
screen being the base of all the presentations on the
screen. This substratum— named *Brahman*, by the
Upanishads— permeates everything in the world. It is
the common content of all that has a name and/or form.
For that very reason. It has no name or form for itself.
It is spoken of as 'THAT' in the neuter gender by the
Upanishads. This is the Unique Godhead of Hinduism.
There is no other. There is no second. It is the source
of all energy, of all power, either in nature or in living
beings. But the difficulty with this concept of Godhead
is this: there is no subject-object relationship in this context, *Brahman* cannot be an object of cognition, since
Brahman has no second. In fact nothing can be predi-
cated about *Brahman* without delimiting the infinite-
ness of *Brahman*. So Hindu Vedanta, with a mathema-

tical precision, has postulated that the moment one wants to think of *Brahman* as an object of thought, one has already delimited *Brahman* and is only thinking of *Iswara*, otherwise called *Saguna Brahman, Brahman* with attributes.

Iswara is the all-powerful Almighty which is the subject of all religions. It has all the supreme qualities of *Brahman*—if *Brahman* can be said to have qualities or attributes—and in addition, it could be the object of our thought process. By its very nature all names and forms suit it. The Vedic logic here is really very subtle, interesting and should be enjoyed as such. It has no name or form and therefore it could be called by any name and could be given any form. The concept of idol worship is the practical implementation of this unique logic of Hinduism. Hinduism has the daring to carry the rationale of this to its logical conclusion and hence it is we find a plethora of 'gods' and 'goddesses' in the Hindu framework. Since no single name or form of God can fully describe the infinite grandeur that is God, since each name and form is only a symbol that points to something that is beyond this visual representation and since each is only a representation of some aspect or manifestation of the supreme Divinity, it is the entire array of all names and forms of God that will approximate to the fullness that is God.

In spite of all this, knowing the weakness of Man, Hinduism recommends that each person may choose his God. This is called the doctrine of *Ishta Devata*, which is another distinguishing feature of Hinduism. If the grossest manifestation is the only thing that suits your taste, or mood or psychological make-up or intellect you are free to worship God in that form. Even the same person may worship an idol at one time and at another

time may meditate and attempt to merge in the transcendental *Para Brahman* which is the basic divine chip
that we are all made of, if we care to look within ourselves. One may choose an ishta devata as per one's
taste and worship that as the Ultimate. It is this train
of thought in the Hindu mind which lives with different *Puranas* extolling different deities. The *Siva Purana*
may say that *Siva* is the greatest God, every other God
is subordinate to it and the *Vishnu Purana* may say the
same thing of Vishnu. There is no contradiction meant,
implied or slurred over. This is the remarkable beauty
of Hinduism. When they say that all Gods are nothing
but names and forms of the same Ultimate *Para Brahman,* they mean it. If you understand it the wrong way,
you are the one to blame, not Hinduism. This is why
when we explain Hinduism to a non-Hindu or to a
novice we have to start from the philosophical end.
Naive explanations of Hinduism without touching the
basic philosophy inherent in everything in Hinduism
not only do not give the truth but they misrepresent
the religion. These naive explanations would crumble
even in the understanding of the *Ramayana* serial on the
TV, because it is shown (rightly) there that on one side
Rama worships *Siva* and on the other side *Siva* worships Rama. When Divinity appears as a physical
manifestation for a specific purpose, for that context,
for that moment, that manifestation is considered to be
supreme. You can therefore choose your *ishta devata* and
worship it exclusively as the Ultimate.

Hindu tradition has mainly six types of *Ishta Devata*
worship which can be listed as the worship of

Aditya, the Sun-God;

Ambika, the Mother-Goddess, in her three forms of
Durga, Lakshmi or *Saraswati;*

Vishnu, belonging to the classic Trinity;

Ganesa, the elephant-faced God, considered as the primal God of all worship;

Maheswara or *Siva,* the third God of the Trinity; and

Subrahmanya, the six-faced God known also as *Kumaran* or *Murugan* in Tamil.

These six are the original subtle manifestations of the *Para Brahman.* The Avatars of *Vishnu,* like Rama and Krishna are more concrete manifestations of the same *Para Brahman.* So they are identified with *Vishnu* in the above list. Every other variation of the *Ishta-Devata* worship may be considered as belonging to one or a combination of these six traditions. In addition the choice of an *Ishta Devata,* instead of being an academic exercise, became a choice of one among the thousands of temples all over the country and the deity chosen may very well be the particular deity enshrined in that particular temple, though belonging to one of the six streams of divinities listed above. It is this variety that gives richness to Hinduism and it is this possibility of 'to each according to his need and capacity' that brings together under the one banner of Hinduism people with varying practices, attitudes and states of evolution. Accordingly carving of images of gods both for worship at home and in the temples became one of the most highly developed art and profession in India. The religious life of India has thus been nourished through the ages on a visual statement, unmatched, perhaps, in the history of any civilization.

Let us now come to the concept of Bhakti in action. Bhakti is built on the plank of faith that there exists a supreme power, in the form of an ultimate godhead, without whose Will there is not even a swing of a little leaf but who is represented by all the different gods and goddesses. There are three stages of Bhakti: *Bahya* Bhakti, *Ananya* Bhakti and *Ekanta* Bhakti. *Bahya* bhakti is external devotion. It assumes that God is external to you, He is in the temples, in bathing ghats, in banyan trees. One feels 'I must go there and worship'. This is a *tamasic* bhakti or unenlightened bhakti. Even this has a place in all religions because it is this popular facet of religion that is visible to the outsider and it is here that faith starts. It is this which gets expressed in processions, festivals and melas. Ananya bhakti, on the other hand, which is categorised as *rajasic* bhakti, is the exclusive devotion of a deity irrespective of anything else. The classic example is that of *Tulsidas*, the author of *Ramcharitamanas*. In every line of this monumental work we find the ananya bhakti of Tulsi reverberating. Not only this. In every line we see the exclusive godhood of Ram as the Ultimate Godhead of Hinduism. To the credit of this type of Bhakti, however, it must be said that never did such bhakti in India lead to intolerance though the dividing line is rather thin between this type of exclusive passionate devotion and bigotry. This is because such devotees are so fully convinced of the all-pervading nature of their God that they really believe that any other god that anybody else worships is only a different manifestation of their own *ishta devata*. This is a welcome spin-off of the philosophical foundations on which Bhakti in Hinduism stands. A Rama *bhakta* like *Tulsi* would sincerely believe that a Jesus or a Buddha is nothing but an Avatar of his Rama and therefore there was no question of any intolerance.

Let us continue with the different stages of Bhakti that we were talking about. The third stage of Bhakti is the noblest stage, the stage of *Satvic* bhakti. It is an ekanta bhakti. It is devotion done purely as a duty to God, expecting nothing in return, in the fullness of God's Love, and living in that Love completely and totally merged in that Love of God. It is a divine ever-flowing love; it is the love of the Gopis to God. It is a self-effacing love, unmatched by any other love or devotion that we know of.

For the ordinary person who may express his bhakti in one of nine ways as elaborated by *Prahlada*, the most important in modern times is that of nama-sankirtana—reciting of God's names and His glories and the majesty of His deeds. We should be indebted to that sage *Vyasa* in this connection because it is in his works, namely, the *Mahabharata* and the *Puranas* we find innumerable stotras that serve as texts for such recitations. (Incidentally, *Vyasa* and *Valmiki* are the two people who have influenced the largest number of people for the longest period of time, in the history of mankind). The well-known *Sahasranamas*, for example, those of *Vishnu*, *Siva* and *Lalita*—to quote only a few—are unexcelled in world literature for their massiveness in praising the glories of God, for their rhythmic sound effect and for the elevating moods which they can generate. He is *Viswam*, indicating God's immanence in everything of the universe that we know of. He is *Vishnu*, because his radiance pervades the firmament and transcends it indicating His transcendence. He is the microcosm, *Anuh*. He is also the macrocosm, *Brihat*. He possesses all qualities, in fact he is a ton of qualities superlative, *Gunabrit*. On the other hand He is devoid of all attributes, *Nirgunah*. You see the same style in these *Sahasranamas* which is the distinctive character-istic of the *Upanishads*. On the one hand they use the superlatives of all the qualities they can think of; on the other hand they use the negation of all the finite things we are capable of imagining. Whether it is this *Sahasranama* or that, it is the same. Listen to a few names from the *Lalita Sahasranama*. She is *niranjana*, faultless; She is *nirlepa*, attachmentless; She is *nirmala*, blemishless; *nitya*, permanent; *nirakara*, formless; *nirakula*, delusionless and therefore capable of removing our delusion and also not reachable by those who refuse to shed their delusion; *nirguna*, attributeless; *nityamukta*, ever-free; *nirvikara*, changeless; *nityasuddha*, ever pure; *nishkarana*, not the effect of any cause, meaning she is Herself the Cause; *nirupadhi*, limitationless; *niraga*, desireless and therefore *ragamathani*, one who can destroy all desires; *nirmada*, one without pride and therefore *madanasini*, one who can vanquish all pride; *nirbhava*, one without birth and death and for this very reason, *bhavanasini*, one who puts an end to the disease of birth and death. It goes on like this endlessly, as it were. A recitation of these in the fullness of the understanding of their meanings is equivalent to recalling the divinity within us and thereby causing the eradication of the non-divine *vasanas* accumulated in our minds.

Once we do that, the Lord assures us that he will not only reveal His presence to us by giving us divine vision but also He will never let us down. Over the centuries there have been innumerable devotees who have exemplified this in their very lives. But even before history started, the mythological names that have become proverbial in this connection cannot but be recalled, if nothing else, for paying our homage in this context of our attempt to understand Bhakti. These names are, for instance, (in the alphabetical order of their names transliterated into English, for want of a better order!): *Ajamila, Akrura, Ambarisha, Arjuna, Bhishma, Dhruva, Drau-*

*padi, Gajendra, Garuda, the Gopis, Hanuman, Jatayu, Laksh-
mana, Narada, Parasara, Parikshit, Prahlada, Radha, Sanan-
dana, Saunaka, Rukmangada, Sudhama, Sugriva, Suka,
Uddhava, Valmiki, Vibhishana, Vidura, Vyasa, and Yasoda.*
The story about each one of them would run to several
pages and if we parents want our children to know anything about Hinduism we should be able to tell them
these stories at bedtime. There is a misguided feeling
that stories about wolves, rabbits and pigges are the
only right things for children. Maybe it is so. But the
mythological stories of Hinduism have a peculiar fas-
cination for children below 8 and it is during that time
all these stories should be told to them. It is at that time
they would believe them. At 18 it would be too late,
but if they had heard about them for the first time before
they were 8, and had been believing them, they would
start asking the right questions at 18; at 28 they would
probably develop a little interest in understanding the
significance of these stories and at 38 they may start
having some faith in them. And it is at 48 they would
start understanding them and cherishing them. We may
hope that at 58, they would themselves start telling
them to their grandchildren with a total commitment!
Whether you like it or not, this is how Hindu tradition
in India has been preserved over the centuries. And if
we want to preserve it in a new continent, let us better
start now. Since Hindu children abroad do not have the
luxury of their grandparents living with them always,
it is the double responsibility of parents of such children to act both as parents and as grandparents for this
purpose.

Leaving mythology aside, we have during historical times numberless devotees of the Lord on the Indian
soil and every one of them has lived an exemplary life
of devotion. Bhakti itself came to be defined by their

actions and pronouncements. No treatise on Bhakti is necessary to be read. We have only to read the biographies of a *Thyagaraja*, an *Appar*, a *Mira*, a *Ramadoss*, a *Kabir* and a *Vedanta Desika*. Every one of their lives would show how devotion finally ends up with the Grace of God being showered on the devotee. That does not mean, however, that the devotee does not suffer in his material life.

In any theory of Grace it is the surrender to God's Will and humility that matter. And we have to surrender by our own free will. Man has the free will to obey or disobey God. The so-called fatalist view in religion is only a fragmentary part of Hinduism. But somehow it has been bloated to a large extent and Hinduism has been accused both from its own votaries and from outside that it emphasizes fate. No. Because of the *Vasanas* we have brought along with us in the journey through several lives, we are born with a particular parentage, in a particular environment and in a particular sex. Our fate is reflected mainly in our tendencies that we have created for ourselves through our past actions. When somebody says, 'I cannot resist having coffee at this particular time', he simply means 'I have taken coffee at this particular time of day every day all my life and so my system is tuned to having it at this time'. An elaboration of this generalised to your past through several of your lives is the *Vasana* theory. Fate does not influence anything else except your tendencies. Everything else is your making in this life. You have total free will to surrender to God or not. But if you surrender to Him with all your heart and soul, He promises that He will take care of your Yoga, security and *Kshema*, well-being. Whosoever offers to Me with love, a leaf, a flower, a fruit or even water, says the Lord, I shall

partake of His offering and bless him. So we have only
to purify the feeling behind every act of worship of ours
in order to win His Grace. And the Lord continues,
whatever you do, dedicate it to Me. Whatever you do
in your daily life, in your annual life, in your special
life, in your official life, in your social life, in your private life, in your internal mental life, dedicate everything to Me and I will do the Magic of purifying them,
says the Lord.

Why can't God give us that feeling of Bhakti? This
is a question which occurs to many of us. God certainly
grants that Bhakti. But we have to receive it. If our
minds are closed, we may not receive it even when it
is pouring. He keeps on pouring His love but very often
we do not look to Him for that Love. Actually He waits
and waits until we take the first step towards Him out
of our own free will. Why should He submit Himself
to this 'agony' of waiting for His children to become
His devotees is one of the mysteries of God. In His
'agony' He grabs you even when you take a simple step
towards Him. He thinks (!) that you have already, like
Thyagaraja, cried to him: *Kalaharana mele ra, ... Dina dina
munu tirigi tirigi dikkuleka saranu jochi tanuvu danamu ni
deyari ...*, meaning: I have wandered day in and day out,
finding refuge nowhere; I have sought your feet and
surrendered myself—body and its possessions—as
your own; why this delay in blessing me? So He grabs
us, even though we have just mildly turned towards
Him, like a blotting paper which the fountain pen has
just touched with the tip of the pen! He consumes us
with His love. But even when we have become His
devotees, we want only petty things from Him and
sometimes He gives us all the petty things we want,
so that in due time we would want what He wants to

give us. All our temples, gods and goddesses and the innumerable ways by which we can propitiate the divine in these places of worship, as well as the uncountable methods of offering our private prayers, with or without the ritualistic *mantras*—all of them have that one objective, that we should ultimately want to go back to where we came from, that is, merge in Him and His glory.

CHAPTER 4

Krishnavatara, the Miraculous

Janamashtami is celebrated all over India and all over the Krishna-Conscious world in the memory of Lord Krishna's birth said to have happened around 5000 years ago. *Vyasa's Mahabharata* is full of Krishna's exploits. But it is in one of his later works, viz., the *Bhagavatam*, that we find a systematic account of the graphic details of Krishna's birth and of his life, which was full of miracles. Any other account of Krishna which was written far later, traces its source to these accounts of *Vyasa*. *Vyasa's* account is therefore the earliest record of one of the oldest events of human history that mankind is remembering and celebrating, year after year. In fact it is the second oldest event of human history, the first one being the birth of Lord Sri Rama. Krishna is remembered by two types of people: the first type being that of the emotional and the sentimental, these are charmed and mesmerised by Krishna's miraculous birth and exploits; the second type being that of the intellectual and the analytic, these are fascinated by Krishna's *Bhagavad-Gita*. This latter shall be our starting point.

It was a major world war, again around 5000 years

ago, in which every king of India was involved. The armies arrayed on either side totalled 18 *Akshauhinis*. One *Akshauhini* is 21870 units, each unit comprising one chariot, one elephant, one horse, five warriors on these and five soldiers on foot. There were 11 *Akshauhinis* on the side of *Duryodhana* and 7 *Akshauhinis* on the side of *Yudhishtira*. Everybody talked of the foremost heroes of the war on either side, *Karna* and Arjuna. The dominant personality throughout the one-month long preparation for the war was Lord Krishna who donated all his armies to *Duryodhana* and stood by himself weaponless, to be the charioteer for Arjuna. On the fateful first day of the War, everything was almost set for the beginning, the first arrows were going to be shot— and right at that time, Arjuna collapsed in total frustration at the sight of his having to fight his own kith and kin, elders and masters, and he threw down his bow and arrow and sat down, refusing to take any step further— in fact wanting to retire to the forest as a *Sannyasi*. Krishna had to use all his miraculous ingenuity to quell the excitement of ignorance and compassion that had arisen in Arjuna's mind. Krishna talks of the great truths of the *Vedanta* embodied in the *Upanishads*, how the Self has nothing to do with what happens to the body and mind, how one has to do his duty, come what may and how the misplaced compassion that has arisen in Arjuna's mind ill becomes him. Arjuna asks several questions, including the million dollar question: If you extol the quality of Detachment and Renunciation so much why are you prodding me to kill? Then comes an elaborate explanation from the Lord on what Karma Yoga means, how actions fulfilled in total desireless attitude do not bind the person, how Karma Yoga is the only resort of mankind since man cannot but keep acting.

And Krishna adds: I have taught this long ago to the Sun-God, who taught it to *Manu*, who taught it to the first king *Ikshvaku* and from whom it has come down from generation to generation. Arjuna suddenly wakes up from his frustrated state of helpessness, becomes his own dynamic self of courage, intelligence and inquisitiveness and asks: You were born just a few years before me. How can it be true that you taught it to the Sun-God and all that? How is it possible? Arjuna behaves at this point like any intelligent rational human being. Till now for the earlier two chapters of the *Bhagavad-Gita* the preacher and his disciple had been talking just like any other teacher and student, just on the academic plane. Arjuna's question shakes off the self-imposed humility, as it were from the Lord, and He replies, in a few of the most inspired *Slokas* of the Gita (IV-5,6,7 and 8):

Bahuni me vyatitani ... ... yuge yuge

Till then, the Gita reads as if it were just an academic thesis on the truths of Hinduism. But at this point, the Gita starts its character as a religious work. In the western world, religion and philosophy are considered to be two isolated independent facets of human activity. But not so in the eastern world of Hinduism, Buddhism and Jainism. Here the daily living of a religious life is based on a philosophical understanding of Man's innate nature. That is why it is very difficult to separate religion from philosophy in our understanding of ancient Hindu traditions. In these Slokas, Krishna declares:

I have gone through many lives and so have you. Whereas I know them all, you don't know

*a thing. Though I am ever unborn, and my Self
is imperishable and though I am Master of all
beings, ruling over My own Nature, out of my
own free will, I manifest myself as a visible
Being. Whenever there is a decline of Dharma
and whenever there is a rise of Adharma, I
incarnate myself for the protection of the Good,
and for the destruction of the wicked, and for
the establishment of Dharma, I create myself,
again and again, yuga after yuga.*

These *Slokas* constitute the *Avatara Rahasya*, the
secret of the concept of Avatar, in the Gita and it has
not come forth so majestically and so powerfully in any
other portion of Hindu religious literature. When Arjuna
asked the question as to how it is possible that Krishna,
who was sitting before him in flesh and blood and who
was just under forty years of age, could have taught
the Sun-God years ago, Arjuna was naturally referring
to that birth of Krishna about which his mother *Kunti*
had told him several times. It was on that *Ashtami* day
after *Sravan Poornima*, when the Moon was in the
asterism *Rohini*—corresponding to the star Aldebaran,
in modern terminology—that Krishna was born in
that famous prison of *Kamsa* of Mathura. According
to the hair-raising description of that birth in the
Srimad Bhagavatam, tenth canto, third chapter, it was
in the dense darkness of that fateful night, the Lord
appeared— mark the word, appeared, not born—as
an unusual child from the womb of *Devaki*, just like the
full moon rising on the eastern horizon!. Oh, what a
sight it was! Continues the *Bhagavatam*:

*Tamadbutam balakam ... ... Vasudeva Aik-
shata. Vasudeva saw that wonder child—*

*with four hands, holding a conch, a mace, a
chakra and a lotus; with Srivatsa emblem on
his chest; with Kaustubha gem on the neck;
with cloth of golden hue; as beautiful as the
blue water-filled cloud; with dense hair flow-
ing around amidst the adornments of crown
and ear-rings radiant with precious gems; and
excellently brilliant with bracelets around the
hip and arms.*

Struck with awe and wonder at the sight, *Vasudeva* praises the Lord and His glory and *Devaki* also joins
him. *Devaki* is naturally scared of the possibilities of
Kamsa hearing of the birth and walking in any moment
to kill the new-born child. So she pleads that the baby
should become a natural baby immediately and she
wants to think of some way of hiding the baby. The Lord
(in the form of the baby) speaks, reminds them of their
previous births, how she and her husband had done a
massive *Tapas* for ages, and the Lord had promised
them that He would incarnate as their issue. And then,
right in front of their view the child assumes a normal
human form and then all the story that we know took
place.

Now let me raise the major question that arises in
the mind of a sceptic or in the mind of the teen-agers
or in the mind of an enquiring intellectual. Was all this
true? Did something like this really happen? Could it
have happened? Is it a historically accurate account that
is written in the book of *Srimad Bhagavatam* or is it the
fantastic imagination of an over-zealous superstitious
fanatic *Vyasa*, who, any way had a vested interest in
promoting his brand of religion? How can we believe
such a thing as a newly born baby with four arms, with

bracelets and anklets, and speaking to its parents in that way? In fact, if we pursue the story further, it says, that the gates of the prison opened themselves for *Vasudeva* to carry the child to the other side of the *Yamuna*, and to exchange it for the other child (the *Yoga Maayaa* as it is referred to in the book) born there in distant *Gokul* and all that story of *Kamsa* coming and getting totally disappointed and scared by the fact that the eighth child had been a female child and even that child would not stay in his hands until he could crush it, and more amazingly, the child speaks from the heavens as it were, to announce that the real killer of *Kamsa* has been born somewhere else already. All this is totally unbelievable, if you approach it from a rational point of view. I hear some of my young readers already saying to themselves—all this fairy tale story is fit only for the kindergarten, but not for us. So let us examine it.

Why don't we want to belive it? Let us analyse this behaviour of our modern mind in a logical manner. There are two kinds of disbelievers of this story. Some people say they believe in God alright, but they are not prepared to take this story as historic. According to them, some well-meaning person, *Vyasa*, perhaps, has invented these stories for purposes of instilling faith in the masses, in our religion. According to them it is not necessary to believe in such stories in order to understand the principles and practices of the ancients. If you ask them whether they believe the words of the Lord himself in the Gita they will have a hard time explaining how they are prepared to take the teaching given in the Gita as Gospel but still they cannot digest the supposedly historical accounts mentioned in the fourth and eleventh chapter of the Gita. The other kind of disbelievers go one step further because they don't believe

in the concept of God itself—much less its Avatar. But
both kinds of disbelievers, if asked to pinpoint their reasons for their disbelief in these stories, would say something like this: One, it is so unnatural, extraordinary and
ridiculous an event to have happened in reality. Two,
it is against scientific spirit and rationale to believe in
something for which you have no convincing evidence
of the kind accepted by modern science. And thirdly,
there is, no documentation of this event which has been
preserved in a scientific way. All these three reasons
and some kind of modifications and combinations of
them exhaust all possible alibis for not believing the
birth of Krishna in the way it is told in the Bhagavatam.

The answer to all these dilemmas is simple. Notice
that every argument that is being given has something
to do with science and scientific rationale. Why do we
bring science and scientific temper into the picture here?
Who told us that God has to behave in a scientific
manner in whatever he does? The concept of God is not
part of science. The existence of God is not a question
that science can answer nor does it want to pose it as
a question for itself. When the existence of God itself
has not been answered by science, what scientific mind
thinks that God, if He exists, has to follow scientific
norms and rationale? How much of God do we know
to assert that he has to behave only this way? Are we
not transcending the limited confines of physical time,
space and matter, which science set for itslef? How can
science help us where it has failed to express itself? In
fact science has been truly scientific in saying that it has
nothing to say on God. Have we ever thought of the
matter that science explains, promises to explain and
hopes to explain only a fragment of what we call the
universe around us and the universe within us? A large

fragment of this knowledge is still untouched by science. Our entire mental universe, for example. Only the great religious leaders, from time immemorial, have ever dared talk about these. Only the *Upanishads* and scriptures of the East have treaded this path. In unravelling the mysteries of our mental universe, we cannot make much progress without getting into deep questions of philosophy, handed down to us by our religions. Science and Religion are two sides of the same coin. Without the two sides there is no coin! More dramatically science and religion are like mother and father to us. In tracing one's genealogy, suppose one refuses to look at the mother's side, what kind of genealogical study would it be? What kind of genetic understanding would it give you if you refused to look at the mother's side? This is what we are doing when we put the emphasis on science and refuse to look at our philosophical heritage and understanding. Let us have a little digression on the complementary roles of science and religion.

While science informs you, religion can transform you. While science describes life, religion explains life. While science caters to your intellect, religion appeals to your intuition. While science unravels the 'what' of things, religion reveals the 'that' of things. While science by its very nature has to be subject to the rationale, religion by its very purpose has to transcend that rationale. While science exploits for you the reductionist aspect of the universe, Hindu religion and philosophy puts together for you the holistic aspect of the universe. While science has made major contributions to the minor needs of man, religion and philosophy have only minor expectations from man for his major needs. While science is a collective obligation, answerable to

the peers in the society, religion is an individual responsibility, irrespective of the experts in the society. While
science takes care of your micro problems, religion and
philosophy undertake to fulfill your macro aspirations.
While the 'micro' is in our scientific hands, the 'macro'
is in His invisible hands!

The concept of Avatar is an ascientific concept and
is one of the most difficult to understand for the modern
mind. The word Avatar comes from the root word
meaning 'to descend'. The *Upanishads* might repeatedly
declare: *Brahman* alone is Truth; it is the all-pervading,
self-luminous Spirit, the final cause of everything in the
Universe; it is a vast ageless boundless ocean of which
everything visible is just only a wave; you and I are only
drops of water in that wave. But however repetitive and
forceful these declarations may be, humanity does not
shed its weakness, its ignorance and take the word of
God. A 'Son of God' has to descend on earth in flesh
and blood and show to the world that He also can take
a name and form as a human being and show mankind how to live their lives. There are two objections
from a rationalist here. One is, if God exists he should
be supercosmic or extracosmic and so should not intervene in the affairs of the world. We agree with the
rationalist that the existence of God has to be postulated.
In fact nothing in this world can be transacted without
some postulation. Even one's father is a father only by
hypothesis, postulated to us, by the mother. To continue,
the rationalist forgets that, having postulated God, he
is contradicting himself. God is not God if He is not
omnipotent. Such an omnipotent God cannot be limited by any of your rules with 'must' and 'should'. The
second objection of the rationalist is: Why should an
omnipotent God who is Master of the entire Universe

who could make anything happen on earth, have to resort to miracles to achieve His objectives,— if He has any, that is.? If He wanted to avoid somebody dying of cancer he could have prevented the man from contracting it in the first place instead of allowing him to contract it and then cure it by a miracle! Why did He create *Kamsa* first, allow him do all the mischiefs that the world could not tolerate and then take the trouble of 'descending' down to Earth in the miraculous way of a Krishna baby and go through all those tortures of struggle with the devil of a *Kamsa* to kill him? The only explanation could be that God creates men with a free will to do what they will but still expects them to behave like human beings out of their own choice; and only when *adharma* increases beyond proportions He decides to intervene.

But again there are Avatars and Avatars. Rama and Krishna were the two most famous Avatars of God but the two were entirely different. Each had its own purpose and its own natural style of behaviour and teachings. Throughout his Avatar, Rama never declares himself God come down on Earth, though the *rishis* of his time believed him to be so. He behaves like an ordinary mortal, but exhibits extraordinary human qualities and lives the life of an ideal man. On the other hand, the Avatar of Krishna loses no time in declaring Himself God on Earth and performs miracle after miracle, almost for the asking. His life is full of apparent contradictions and only the really blessed ones recognize Him as the manifestation of the Supreme Lord. And even they at crucial times are so blinded by the divine *Maya* that they treat Him like an ordinary child or an ordinary person. Coming to our own times we have it on the authority of the personal experience of

several devotees that fully evolved beings like Ramakrishna, Sri Aurobindo, Ramana Maharshi and Kanchi
Kamakoti Sankaracharya the eldest, cannot but be
manifestations of the Supreme Divinity. Each of these
had their own style and purpose. But the question arises:
If all these are avatars of Divinity, why have all the problems of this suffering world not been solved? Why are
people still suffering? If God has come down on Earth,
why does He allow suffering to continue? Why do we
fight before His very eyes? These questions were
already posed and answered in the book 'Essentials of
Hinduism'. We quote below extracts from the answers
on pages 100 and 101 of the book:

"The descent of Divinity on Earth is to establish
faith in the existence of a higher reality and the truth
of spiritual laws, so that we may have the strength to
turn towards *Dharma* and steadfastly work for our salvation. If the Supreme Reality in the form either of the
omnipotent Divinity or an Avatar solved all our problems of poverty, disease, fear and hate, do you think
that would be the end of our problems? The cure of our
bodily illnesses or of our poverty would still leave us
at the same level of consciousness and spiritual evolution as before, so that, very soon, we would again be
at one another's throats and the same chaotic world
would continue."

While walking along the shores of the Arabian Sea
somebody asked Sri Sathya Sai Baba: Why don't you
change this entire sea into a sea of oil and then all eco-
nomic problems of India would be solved?! And quickly
came the reply: Supposing it is done, who will give me
the guarantee that no crazy man would throw a lighted
cigarette in that sea of oil?! Not even God can give that

guarantee, because man has the free will to do what he likes.

"If God had really a purpose in descending on Earth, it could not be to solve our mundane problems of illness and poverty. It would be to clear the way for our spiritual growth. But even when an avatar comes, if it comes at all, we may not recognize it or respect it. The only way we may recognize it is through the awareness of certain miracles happening before our very eyes. The purpose of a miracle, from the view-point of Divinity, is not to prove itself, because Divinity has no purposes. Miracles are just a natural outflow of God's Infinite Love for His children. If, in the process, we are attracted towards Him, we should only be more thankful to Him for allowing us to witness His *Leela*.. The Lord Himself declares in effect: 'My *Maya* is incomprehensible to the human mind. Don't try to understand it intellectually. You can never do that. But pray for my Grace which will help you transcend that'. In this process of worship and prayer, in order to strengthen your faith, He sometimes grants you things which are just mundane and trivial from the spiritual point of view. There is however nothing wrong in praying to God for the solution of your difficulties. What is important is not what you want but whom you ask for its fulfillment. The Avatar comes down on Earth to remind you of these truths and turn you inward.' And whatever Avatar one considers none can deny the fact that whoever that came into even remote contact with that Avatar did change to a higher level of evolution.

CHAPTER 5

Hinduism—Attitudes, not Rituals

Hinduism is a multifaceted religion with a wide spectrum of norms and practices and a lot of flexibility in terms of rules and regulations. This has been very often overplayed to such an extent that an intelligent observer either from the inside or the outside finds it difficult to clearly lay down what is right and what is wrong in any given set of circumstances. The scriptures and the authorities are so many and so varied that a passing acquaintance will only see a bundle of contradictions, and traditions that, on the face of it, are nothing but a totality of superstitions. The purpose of this chapter shall be to present the thesis that it is always the attitude with which one approaches his task that matters irrespective of the physical situation or the ritualistic norms or the external manifestation of the action involved.

Let us first take the aspect of rituals in Hinduism. There are rituals in every religion. Perhaps, if there were no rituals, it would not be a religion! Even in our ordinary world of external activities, is not a vote of thanks a ritual? Would the civilized world vote for a permanent abolition of the ritual of a vote of thanks? On the other hand, haven't we observed that even a vote of thanks, in the hands of a competent person can become an enjoyable and refreshing affair instead of a 'mere ritual'? Rituals in Hinduism, if done in the right spirit, can serve as an entry point to the world of the spirit. Just as you have to fill up various forms to get anything done in the civilized world, rituals are the forms you must fill in order to carry on in the spiritual world. Neither rituals, nor penances, nor purificatory rites by themselves can deliver the goods. Penances and purificatory rites are prescribed for only those who have turned away from sin. They come in only after the change of heart. They are a mark that one is retracing one's steps away from one's evil ways. They serve to show repentance. This is what *prayas-chitta* means. No scripture implies that sin could be removed by means of distribution of gifts or observance of fasts without an antecedent change of heart. If they had, they would not have prescribed many instances of 'substitute' *prayas-chittas*. Just one classical instance. We quote from the book 'Essentials of Hinduism', p. 20:

"A *Krichhracharana* is an observance prescribed by the *Smritis* for the expiation of several types of sins. It consists of twelve days of observance, eating only one day-meal for the first three days and nights, only one night-meal for the next three, and eating only food brought by a third person, voluntarily and unasked, for the next three and finally, complete fasting for the last three days and nights. This constitutes one *krichhra*. If a person observed these continuously through a cycle of 1080 *krichhras*, the *Smriti* says, the totality of one's sins through all one's previous lives would be wiped out! The full observance would thus run over 36 years. Now comes the important point. 'If one cannot perform this continuous *Krichhracharana* for 36 years, 'the *Smriti* continues, 'he may do it for 12 years, or if even that is impossible, he may do it for six years, or in the alternative, for three years, or in the final alternative, for one year'! If one year would suffice, why first of all start with a prescription of 36 years, which is almost an impossibility? It is clear that what matters is not the action but the attitude which one brings to bear in performing it. If the change of heart that motivates the observance for as long as 36 years can be sufficiently intensified over a period of even one year, then that would be enough. This must be the spirit of the *Smriti* injunction.''

That it is the attitude that is always important rather than the physical action, can be substantiated by several illustrations and points of view. The simplest illustration is that of a one-year old child kicking its mother with its feet. The mother almost enjoys it. But suppose it were a twenty-year old 'child'! The mother would look for various reasons and if the circumstances even remotely fit them, she is going to take strong objection and perhaps leave the 'child' in protest. It is the attitude that matters. In the case of the adult 'child' with no mental complaint, the attitude of innocence or fun is not acceptable. Thus though the action is the same, the difference in attitude makes all the difference.

Sage Sri Ramakrishna has given us a telling story which illustrates the importance of attitudes in a dramatic way. There was a devout *Sannyasi* carrying on his daily duties of preaching, living in a village. Right opposite to his abode or *Ashram*, there happened to live a lady, who had no other occupation except to sell her body. But the lady was really repentant. She certainly did not like her profession, and so was always mentally cursing herself for this. In fact her mind constantly turned towards the opposite house where not a day passed without a *Satsang* or a *Bhajan* or a *pravachana* by the *Sannyasi*. She was almost mesmerised by the sequence of events in the *Ashram* opposite and she wreathed in agony that she could not participate in them. On the other hand, look what was happening to the *Sannyasi*. He knew that the opposite house was a house of sin. His compassionate mind also wreathed in agony that the lady could be moving headlong in her downward path of spiritual devolution. His compassion involved him to such an extent that he even kept track of how many persons visited the opposite house every day and he wanted to pray to God for her reformation and salvation. In order perhaps that his prayers may be specific for her and her clients, he did not, even for a moment, take his eyes (and mind!) off the opposite house. Well, there comes a day of reckoning for everything. It happenend that both of them died on the same day. The angels took her to heaven whereas he, the *Sannyasi*, was taken to a terrible hell. The *Sannyasi* protested: 'What are you doing to me? Why are you taking me to hell? I have been nothing but a *Sannyasi* all through my life. I know how much sinful the opposite house prostitute has been. And it boils my blood to see you are taking her to heaven. This is a crime against *Dharma*'. In answer to his continued protests like this, they took him to their Master in heaven and the latter explained to him: Look what is happening to her body with which she committed all her sin. It is being stoned by the villagers and dragged into the sewage. Whereas, your body, which did very noble things, is being garlanded by all the villagers and taken out in procession with pomp and glory. Her soul goes to heaven because that is what she deserves for all her repentance and her total mental identification with the spiritual practices happening in your *Ashram*. Whereas, you mentally identified yourself with each one of her activities to such an extent that your mind was not in the "noble" work you were outwardly carrying on. For your attitude of being immersed in filth all through your life, this is what you deserve!

Always it is the attitude that matters. A judge who punishes a criminal with death sentence is not considered to have sinned, just because it is an attitude of duty and dedication to the laws of the land that makes him give the death sentence and not that of a revengeful victim or bystander of the crime. An idol, when it is worshipped, is not worshipped as an idol. It is worshipped with the attitude of a devotee in the presence of God Himself. It is God who is worshipped in the form of the idol. Since God can be in any form and can have any name, worshipping the idol with the attitude of being in the presence of Divinity is more commendable than closing the eyes supposedly in meditation of that Divinity but really thinking of all earthly distractions. Once we have that attitude and awareness of God's presence, God will really be present there. it is that firm conviction of *Prahlada* that made him say with extreme confidence that He is everywhere and certainly in this pillar and lo and behold, the Lord did come out of the pillar and vindicate his devotee. The story of Kannappa Nayanar again goes to show how important is the attitude of devotion, in spite of what it might appear in its external manifestation. Kannappar was totally a rural uncivilised hunter in a forest who became enlightened by just seeing the linga of Kalahasti in the Andhra region. He knew not how to ritually worship the Lord. Of the need for external purity while offering worship, he had not even an inkling. He offered meat to the Lord, and that too, first tasted by him. He committed several other 'sacrileges'. But his devotion was so pure, that the Lord performed a miracle before the temple priest to show the divinity of Kannappar's Bhakti. It was demonstrated how, losing one eye already, he was prepared to offer the other eye also to the Lord, and in order to be able to locate the position of the eyes of the Lord after he himself would have lost both his eyes he kept track of the eye of the Lord by keeping his foot on the face of the Lord. These 'sacrileges' were all excused by the Lord because of the intensity of Kannappar's Bhakti and it was this intensity which made Sankara himself write about it as a model for Bhakti in every sense of the word. Kannappar's story would not have any validity if we did not go by 'attitudes' in the interpretation of religion.

Here is a very interesting story told by Sri Sathya Sai Baba on the need to have a hundred per cent faith. Such a total faith will certainly be rewarded by the Lord. The story is told of a certain devotee who wanted something very specific from the Lord. He met a *Sadhu* who advised him to worship Lord *Siva* elaborately every day in a ritualistic fashion. The devotee was following the instructions closely for a whole month but nothing happened in terms of the Grace of the Lord showing forth or anything. Another *Sadhu* passed by and seeing this devotee carrying on his worship so steadfastly, the *Sadhu* enquired and found out the truth. He offered an unsolicited advice and said: *Siva* is not the God to propitiate for such kinds of prayers to the Lord. After all, *Siva* himself is a pauper and so you better propitiate Lord *Vishnu* who has got Goddess *Lakshmi* as His consort. He will give you what you want. So that *Siva* picture was put away in a corner and the *Puja* of Lord *Vishnu* started in all seriousness. Another month passed by and nothing happened. A third *Sadhu* came along. The devotee went and reported to him and complained that the Lord had not blessed him yet. This *Sadhu* now gave his own advice and said: *Vishnu* and *Siva* are after all only at the mercy of the all-powerful *Sakti*. The Mother Goddess is the store of energy for all these other gods and so it is Her that the devotee should worship. She will definitely grant him what he wanted. So from that day both the *Vishnu* and the *Siva* pictures were put away. The picture of the Mother Goddess adorned the centre of the *Puja* room and very elaborate worship continued for several days. The days were not different and nothing happened to indicate that the Goddess was satisfied. One day at the end of the *Puja*, the devotee was elaborately performing the *Dhupa* ritual, that is, the burning of the incense for the picture of the Goddess. The whole room was filled with incense smoke and he found that the smoke not only covered the picture of the Goddess but it also blocked out the pictures of the Gods *Vishnu* and *Siva* on the wall, which by the way he had pushed to the two corners after his earlier disenchantment with them. The devotee was really furious. How can these discarded gods inhale the incense which he really meant only for the *Sakti* picture in the centre?. He would not allow it. So thinking, he took up two pieces of cloth, covered the two pictures of *Vishnu* and *Siva* so that they cannot inhale the incense and then continued his propitiation of the Goddess. Lo and Behold, it was at that time, the Lords *Vishnu* and *Siva* appeared before him from nowhere. Imagine his consternation and wonder!. He asked them: How come, You Gods did not appear before me when I propitiated you individually each for a month with all that elaborate *Puja*, but now when I have discarded you, you are coming before me when my worship is intended for somebody else? And they replied: That is where our secret lies. The moment you have a firm conviction that we are present here in this room in flesh and blood it is our *Dharma* to present ourselves. When you covered our pictures with cloth so we may not inhale the incense offered to the Goddess, at that time you really believed that we were sitting here inhaling your incense and all that. Whenever a devotee has such an unshaking faith and awareness about our presence, we cannot but be present in person there! It is our *Dharma*. That shows how a hundred percent faith helps. *Prahlada's* faith was of that kind and no doubt the Lord appeared before him.

In Hinduism you can explain everything in terms of the need to have the right attitudes. In fact if we understand this as the central requirement of Hindu religion, we can understand the Gita itself correctly and how it not only taught Arjuna to go back and fight but how it can be our unfailing guide in almost every problem in life. Three articles in the Hindu of Madras on January 10, March 21 and June 13, (1989) elaborately discussed the question of how to interpret the Gita so that it still applies to the issues of modern management without making the Gita contradict what appear to be the norms of result-oriented management techniques. Once we are convinced it is the attitude that matters in Hinduism, and it is the attitude of detachment rather than detachment itself that the Gita propagates, everything would fall in place. There are several stanzas in the Gita which will substantiate this. Every time it talks about relinquishing or renouncing, it discourages the physical act of such renunciation as much as it encourages the mental act of donning an attitude of non-attachment. It is the attachment (*Sanga*) that has to be shunned, avoided, conquered and totally renounced. There is not even a single exception to this in the whole of the Gita. We shall run through some of the relevant portions quickly.

Fixed in Yoga, perform your duties, having relinquished attachment and having become indifferent to failure and success. (II-48). Man does not reach Perfection, merely by renunciation of action (III-4). Always efficiently do your duty without attachment. Doing work without attachment man attains the Supreme. (III-19). As the unwise do actions with attachment, so should the wise man, seeking maintenance of world order act without attachment. (III-25). He who has subdued his mind and body, who has given up all proprietory craving for possessions (and therefore) has no craving—performing sheer bodily action, such a person does not incur sin. (IV-21). Renunciation and Karma Yoga both lead to Supreme Bliss. Of the two however Karma Yoga is superior to renunciation. (V-2). He who acts, offering all actions to God and shaking off attachment, remains untouched by sin, as the lotus leaf by water. (V-10). Yogis perform action, for self-purification, only with their senses, mind, intellect and body as well, but without attachment. (V-11). The self-controlled one, renouncing all actions mentally, rests happily in the city of nine gates, doing nothing or causing nothing to be done. (V-13). An action enjoined by the scriptures, which is done as a duty, giving up attachment (and therefore), and the fruits thereof, that alone is regarded as *satvic* form of relinquishment. (XVIII-9). Mentally surrendering all actions to me ...(XVIII-57)

Each one of these, and in fact the entire Gita, emphasizes the mental attitude of detachment and renunciation rather than a ritualistic renunciation or running away from duty or responsibility. Interpreted in terms of modern management, what all this means is that at every stage of response to the need to act, man, whether he is a manager or a boss or employee, the technique is that of non-attachment to the egoistic feelings that 'I am doing this', 'I must get this done', 'I must push them to do this, otherwise they will not do it', 'It is my plan, I must get it accepted', 'I will not listen to any objections, I have thought out all the possibilities', 'I must push them to do this, otherwise they will not do it', 'It is my plan, I must get it accepted', 'I will not listen to any objection, I have thought out all the possibilities', 'I am the man on the spot, people at the top cannot get to the bolts and nuts as well as I can' ... and so on. In every one of these examples, may be what is being said or thought out by the person concerned is wholly true, but it is the attitude that is wrong. If we can convert each one of these attitudes into one of humility, dedication to the cause, and surrender to the Will of a power above us, then each one of these statements would be dressed up in the cloth of insulation made up of the silk of divinity and then that will not get contaminated by selfishness. The moment the manager thinks that it is not he that is doing what he is doing but it is He that is giving him an oportunity to do what he seems to be doing, his own attitude to his subordinates would change to the extent that they begin to count him on their side instead of a ruthless boss who is always on the opposite side. The moment the employee can brainwash himself into an attitude of dedication to his organization, the idea that somebody is pushing him to do work would vanish. The concepts of dedication and surrender can do a great alchemy which has to be experienced to be believed.

Man should always remember: 'What I do depends
on me; that I do does not; it depends on Him'. This has
been repeatedly emphasized in the Gita. But before we
go to the Gita let us clearly understand what this cryp-
tic sentence means. This has something to do with the
way Fate and Free will have to be interpreted in Hinduism. I have the freedom and the free will to live my
life the way I like. But to live or not there is no freedom for me; it is not in my hands. It is in God's hands.
I can breathe whatever air I like—be it healthy, be it
drugged, be it alcoholic, be it cigarette smoke. But
whether I breathe or not is in His hands. The 'what' is
in my hands. The 'that' is not! Take a simple dramatic
example. I decide to murder somebody. It is my decision. I plan hard, I create an alibi for myself. I go about
plugging all loopholes. I protect myself doubly and
trebly. I have the pistol in my hand. He is alone with
me. I pull the trigger and lo! he does not die, it certainly
hit him but God only knows, why finally he survived.
We can imagine hundred situations how such a thing
could happen. The fact that I have planned for his
murder and have actually pulled the trigger with intent
to kill is against me and I am going to be punished for
this. Because all these were my actions out of my own
free will. On the other hand if I had only accidentally
pulled the trigger, say, in a scuffle, and even if he had
died, I will not be given the punishment which a wilful
murderer will get. That is Law. I am punished for my
attitude and intent and not for the actual event which
followed. What I do is my responsibility. But that I do
it is His Will. In the Gita this is declared by the Lord
in several places but the most dramatic proclamation
comes in the eleventh chapter when He shows Arjuna
His cosmic form and says among other things: 'I have

already slain them all, *Drona, Bhishma, Jayadratha,* and *Karna* and others. Be merely an instrumental cause, O Arjuna, go and fight them and conquer them' (XI-33, 34)

Even at the philosophical heights of Hinduism, it is the attitude that is emphasized. What is *Advaita,*— non-duality? That there is only One Absolute Truth, everything else is only the same in a camouflaged form and name, there is no second,—all these are highest truths of Hinduism and they are taken as the chief plank on which the Advaita philosophy rests its entire edifice. But now, can you practise advaita in physical reality? Can you physically hold the other man as yourself? What about his possessions? What about everything he calls his? What about his spouse?! It is only *Bhava-advaita* (*Advaita* in attitude) that is recommended, not *Kriya-advaita* (*Advaita* in action). Any careful reader of Sankara would recognise this. Otherwise he would not have gone from place to place and worshipped and praised the Divinities that are present there.

To conclude, Man's needs to act are of three kinds. They are: To answer a social purpose; Or to respond to a call of duty; Or to pursue and enjoy a personal gain, tangible or otherwise. Every need for man to act can be put into one of these categories. And in all these cases, his action response would be either born out of his own dynamism, or out of an emotive attachment to a father figure or out of an intellectual reasoning and conceptual conviction or out of an empirical and experimentational methodology. (See Chart). The strategy of the Gita for the first type of response is the attitude of detachment coupled with dedication to a Cause, secular or religious. This is Karma Yoga. The strategy for the second is that of dedication and surrender to the

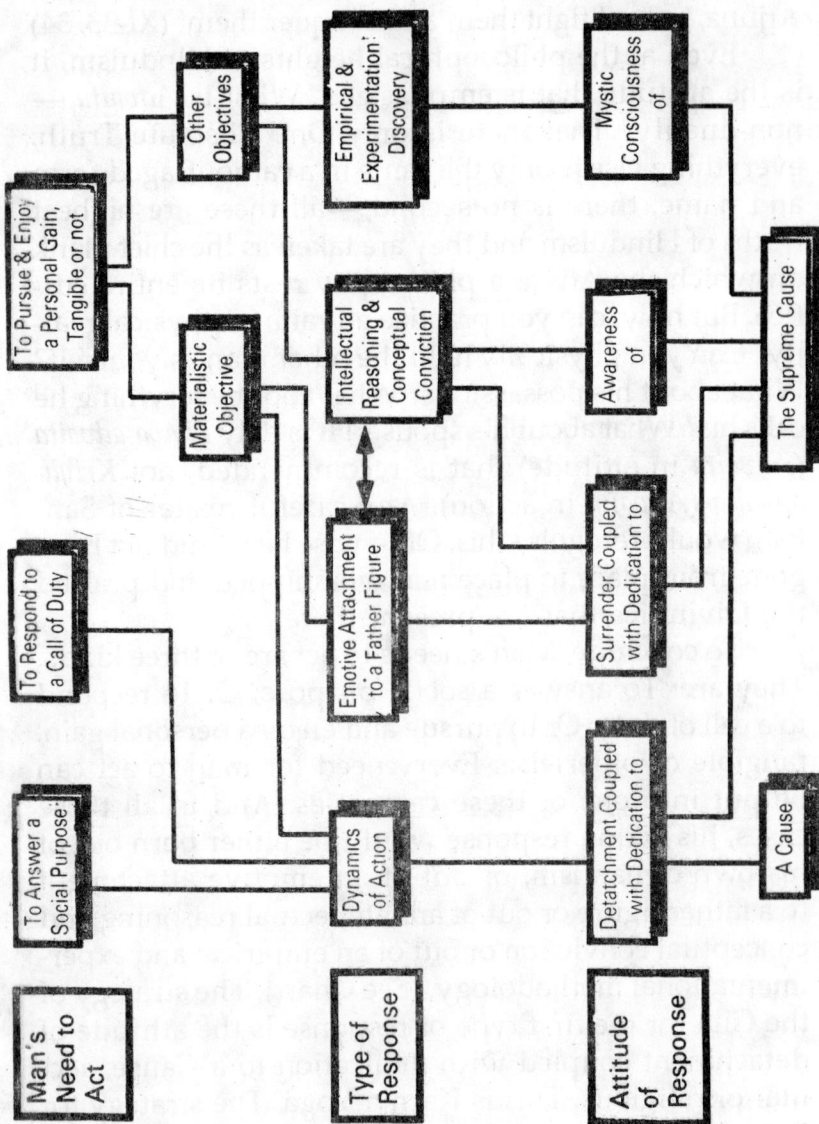

To Pursue & Enjoy a Personal Gain, Tangible or not

To Respond to a Call of Duty

To Answer a Social Purpose

Man's Need to Act

Other Objectives

Materialistic Objective

Empirical & Experimentation; Discovery

Intellectual Reasoning & Conceptual Conviction

Emotive Attachment to a Father Figure

Surrender Coupled with Dedication to

Detachment Coupled with Dedication to

Dynamics of Action

Type of Response

Mystic Consciousness of

Awareness of

The Supreme Cause

A Cause

Attitude of Response

Supreme Cause. This is Bhakti Yoga. That one for the third is the attitude of an awareness of the Supreme Omnipresence. This is *Jnana* Yoga. The last one is answered by the attitude of a mystic consciousness of that Supreme Reality. This is *Raja* Yoga.

CHAPTER 6

What it is to Live as a Hindu?

Even the insiders in Hinduism do not usually know what is right at any given point of time or in any given circumstance. This is because there is too much of flexibility in the norms and practices of the religion and too many varieties of rules and regulations. What are the essentials that should occupy the attention of the practising Hindu? What is the minimum that should be protected for the next generation in terms of observances, attitudes and the ways of life? Can these things be passed on to the next generation in a meaningful way, meaningful to the younger generation, particularly those of the younger generation who are bred and brought up in an environment where they have no impact of their own religion on them? Can the ways of Hinduism be explained to them in a language which makes sense to them in their modern context?

Hinduism is not simply a religion in the sense that there are several religions in the world and they all speak of God, soul, morality, merit versus sin, mortality versus immortality, good versus bad, heaven versus hell and ways of living so that ultimately one reaches salvation. Hinduism is an Action Plan for how to live in peace and die in peace. Hinduism bereft of this action plan for one's daily life is nothing but a bundle of academic and esoteric adventures in human thought, though remarkable for their profundity. These adventures in thinking are all recorded in the great scriptures called *Upanishads*. But since they are very abstract they will not have any impact on you until you have related them to the context of your daily living. When we say that Hinduism is an action plan for daily living so that one can live in peace and die in peace, we do not mean that one should retire from all the dynamism of life and its challenges in the vibrant external world of activity. Hinduism has a unique way of allowing you to be in the midst of your activity and still keep your cool. This they do by recommending what they call Karma Yoga, elaborately explained in the Gita, which is the one scripture for us that bridges our worldly finite interests and intelligence and the philosophical infinities and wisdom of the *Upanishads*.

One major difficulty with the religion of Hinduism is that you cannot expect to understand it in bits and pieces. For everything in Hinduism a proper understanding comes only in the context of a global perception of the entire gamut of the religion. This global perception is what is explained in the *Upanishads*. Essentially it says that the innermost core of every human being, the micro of the micro in him, is divine. The baser instincts of man come from the mind which has accumulated them through its several lives of association with this particular soul. These accumulated imprints of the mind are called *vasanas*. The eradication of all *vasanas* is what makes for release from *Samsara*, the cycle of births and deaths. All the prescriptions of Hinduism are intended to help the mind rid itself of all its load so that in that pure mind God will reflect Himself. The

numberless impurities of the mind act like an indeli-
ble coating on the mind and hide the presence of
the divinity within. All our rules and regulations for
our daily life are programmed to inculcate a habit in
us which would be consistent with the ultimate
requirement of cleaning our mind from all its dirt. What
is dirt? The Samskrit word for dirt is *'mala'*. It is also
used to denote faeces. The latter is a thing which we
refuse to identify with ourselves. In fact in Hindu metaphysics, an object is said to have dirt when it has in it
something other than itself. So a dirtless mind is a mind
which does not contain anything other than the mind!
That mind is the crystalline mind in which God will
reflect Himself. All our religious habits are so programmed and designed that, when the time comes for
us to look godward instead of outward, we shall not
have to unlearn any of our habits. Since the mind is like
a storehouse of everything that has gone into it (for several lives, though now present only in a subtle manner
in the form of *vasanas*), and this storehouse cannot be
emptied by the pressing of a single button, the only way
the mind can be purified and made 'dirtless' is by dilut-
ing its contents by constantly pouring in noble, elevated
thoughts and those thinking processes which are concordant with the upward path to divine perfection. This
is the ultimate purpose of all rituals, ceremonies, observances and penances. It is for this purpose that two great
methodologies, which go by the name of Karma Yoga
and Bhakti Yoga are prescribed and elaborately enun-
ciated in our scriptures. Yoga is efficiency in implementation. *Yogah Karmasu Kausalam* is what the Gita
says. So Karma Yoga means the efficient way of carrying on our activities. Bhakti Yoga means the efficient
methodology for devotion and worship. These are the

two paths that have been shown to lead the average man out of his prison which he has created for himself.

Karma Yoga centres around disinterested unselfish action. It uses the word 'detachment' in this connection. Detachment is non-attachment to the ephemeral and transient things of the world—which include the entire universe, our body, mind and intellect. The one thing that is ever permanent is the substratum of existence that lies at the base of all these things as their root cause, as the canvas on which they are all painted. As the innermost core of our very selves it is called *Atman* and as the utmost transcendent reality which lies beyond anything finite it is called *Brahman*. Now Karma Yoga says: Since there is nothing else other than Atman that is permanent do not be attached to anything that is non-permanent; because that way you will always be open to unhappiness. Happiness is only within you, namely, in the recognition that you are the *Atman* and not this body, mind or the intellect. Once this intellectual understanding of this is granted, then all the unhappiness and miseries of the world can be traced to the fact that we are attached to transient things like our body, our kith and kin, our opinions, our actions and their consequences. The Gita says: Act in the living world by standing apart from it. You may have possessions but be not attached to them. Just as in a play in which you are only one of the actors and all the property you are handling really belongs to the Producer-Director of the play so also understand that in this drama of life all the things you possess, you inherit, you enjoy, you create, or you destroy are not yours but His, namely the Super-Director who is the Supreme Almighty of the Universe. Do your actions certainly as efficiently as you can, as if you are an actor on the stage acting your part well.

In real life for you to get this feeling of detachment, the Gita gives you a strategy of action, namely
that of dedication. Dedication to what? Gita says: dedicate all your actions to God. If you have reservations
in believing in a God, or if you do not understand the
concept of God sufficiently to be able to dedicate your
actions to Him, then you may dedicate your actions to
a Cause which you hold sacred. Or, dedicate everything
to One living Person whom you respect, revere and
adore, like your mother. Accepting suffering for the
happiness of others is dedication. Dedication means that
you do a certain action because the god of your dedication would like it to be done that way and you avoid
doing a certain thing because the god of your dedication would not like you doing that thing. Thus you
totally submit yourself to the will of your god of dedication and all your actions are governed by your own
understanding of what your god of dedication would
accept and not accept. Other than this one desire of
pleasing the god of your dedication you have no desires
of your own., Once you start living your life in such
a dedicatedly streamlined way you will see that your
own mind will have no selfish desires and every action
that you do becomes an unselfish act. You may have
hopes and fears but the joys of one and the burden of
the other are both transferred to the god of dedication
as far as you are concerned. This is Karma Yoga. Gita
says that one who does his actions in this unselfish way
is uncontaminated even if the action itself is harmful
to somebody else. It is like a judge sentencing a criminal to death because the sentence has been given by
the judge with an attitude of total dedication to the Law
of the Nation. You may find it difficult to believe that
this can happen. But you should experiment with this

in your daily life before you pass judgment on this method. The method of dedication will induce an alchemy in all your thought processes and this alchemy will slowly change your personality itself in its upward path of evolution.

Bhakti Yoga implies the recognition of the Supreme Cosmic Power without the sanction of which not even the smallest movement can take place in the universe. This Supreme Power manifests itself in the form of one of several divinities. But when we worship any one of them it is with the conscious understanding that it is the One Almighty God, *Iswara*, that is being worshipped in this form. This is the rationale of idol worship. Another main reason that different gods and goddesses have arisen in Hinduism is the following. In the long mythological history of Hinduism several manifestations of the Absolute Divinity have taken place. Every one of these manifestations had a name and a form and this particular representation of that nameless divinity had caught the imagination of people and they have been worshipped ever since. Not only this. In India, every temple of olden times had arisen like this. Though the physical environs of these large temples have been built in historic times by historical personages, the deity enshrined in the sanctum sanctorum very often goes back in origin to mythological times when that deity really appeared as a manifestation for a specific purpose. There is no other culture in the world whose literature is so fully replete with myriads of such manifestations of divinity and the exploits of that Supreme Almighty for the benefit of His devotees. This is not to say that Indians have been the most religious or devoted, among all the civilisations of the world. It is only to say that India's past goes beyond the few millenia into which history dares peep into. India's past is so ancient and goes back to several millions of years that these events that have been recorded in the form of deities represented in various temples have been discarded by history as belonging to mythology. For instance, the deity, *Nataraja*, of the temple of Chidambaram, where Lord *Siva* had blessed His devotees *Patanjali* and *Vyagrapada* with His Cosmic Dance cannot be dated historically. Carbon dating and other scientific methods can apply only to the physical matter connected witht the temple structure. It can in no way affect the concept enshrined in the temple that motivated the building of the temple and this concept is older than anything that history can speak of. There are innumerable temples that baffle us like this in the entire Indian subcontinent. Every non-resident Indian, in addition to exposing his chi dren to books that speak about India, its culture and its temples, should also be able to take them, with pride, through the length and breadth of the country mainly to look at and understand the concept and mythology behind the several temples in India. The multitude of temples where we find ourselves in the presence of a fantastic atmosphere of architecture, sculpture, frescoes, exuberance of idols, the calm serene times when the temples are isolated, and in contrast the plethora of festivals with the glamour of celebration, majesty, pomp, crowd and noise—all these cannot but have a cultural impact on the children. It is unfortunate that when such tours are attempted, the parents sometimes leave the children behind because of various real and imaginary inconveniences, allegedly to the children, but in reality to themselves.

Besides the ritualistic *Puja* which is the classical expression of an individual's Bhakti, the most well known expression is that of *Namasankirtana*, collective

or individual. The repetition of God's names can be very
rewarding in terms of an elevation of the mood and the
spiritual awakening of the mind. In Samskrit one finds
that every proper name has a meaning. It is usually a
meaning that is derived from the root syllables that go
into the name. To repeat the names of God is to be
immersed in the ecstasy of identity with the glories of
God as encompassed by the name we chant.

He is *Siva* because He is the auspicious among the
auspicious. *Pavitranam pavitram* is the scripture. He is
Sankara because He gives you the ultimate auspicious-
ness, He makes you happy. He is *Kesava* because *kah*
means *Brahma; ha* means *Vishnu;* and *Isah* means *Rudra*
and *kah + Isah + ah* gives the meaning: The One of whom all
the three Gods of the Trinity are only subtle manifestations. He is *Krishna* because He attracts everybody;
also because 'Krs' stands for existence and 'na' stands
for bliss and so Krishna stands for the union of the two.
He is *Narayana* because He pervades all appearances
that come out of the five elements. He abides in them
and they in Him. *Nara* is Atman and from it arose all
the five elements, the effects and these are *naaras.* He
pervades them as their cause, both the efficient cause
and the material cause; because He is the one who
brought them into existence and He is also the one who
Himself became the effects or appears as the effects.
Therefore He is *Narayana.* He is *Vishnu* because He pervades everywhere. The root syllable for *Vishnu* is 'to
pervade'. He is *Rama* because the two syllables 'ra' and
'ma' indicate one in whose memory men revel in joy
and happiness, because *Brahman* itself is indicated by
the word Rama and *Brahman* is the source of all happiness. The syllable 'ra' erases all impurities of the mind
whereas the syllable 'ma' insulates the mind from any

further impurities. It was because of the importance of the name that *Sage Vasishta* chose that name for the godly son of *King Dasaratha*. The name 'Rama' is more important than the character 'Rama' of the *Ramayana*. There is no end to the depth of meanings which are succinctly embedded in the myriads of names of God that Hinduism and the Samskrit language are capable of. The entire gamut of Hindu religion and philosophy goes into these names.

Now let us come to the ultimate purpose of Bhakti Yoga. It is the attainment of Grace from the Lord of worship. Grace does not mean that God is sitting up there in the heavens watching every one of your thoughts and movements and is dispensing justice by His moods of pleasure and displeasure. No. God is in the innermost recesses of our hearts. He resides in us as declared in Sloka 61 of the 18th chapter of the Gita. As a permanent resident in our hearts He knows our sincerity and anguish. His response to the worship is very often an overflowing of His ever-present Love to His children, irrespective of the external characteristics of the devotion. He does not calculate the value of the things you offer Him, He only values the feeling behind your offering. It is only the attitude that matters. Grace is overflowing of the Divine Love into the devotee's heart which is crystalline pure. It is in such crystalline purity that Divinity shows its own reflection. Ultimately whether it is Karma Yoga or Bhakti Yoga, it is the attitude with which you are appraching your task that matters and which decides whether what you are doing is dharma or adharma. Any secular or religious action, if it is done without an iota of selfishness or desire for gratification, in a spirit of detachment, dedication and surrender, will in due course become a habit with you or your way of life and this is what Hinduism wants from you. Now this means tremendous self-discipline. Those of us who have strong will perhaps can attempt this self-discipline ourselves. But those of us who do not have such strong will would rather seek divine help and appeal to Him for success in this attempt at self-discipline. In secular life, particularly, the attitude of surrender to the Supreme Will of the Divine, the attitude of dedication to the cause of the organization that we work for or that we own (by His Grace!) and an absence of egoism from everything that we do, including the management of our subordinates or employees —these are the ways in which our religious attitudes have to be transmitted into our daily worldly life.

Whether it is the secular part or the religious part of our lives, one has to start by changing one's attitude to daily matters of life. The control of the mind, which is the fundamental thing to attempt is a never-ending war with oneself. In this war, the only thing that helps is to keep close to the source of all strength, energy and power in the world, namely God. The attitude of an undercurrent of awareness of the omnipresence of God is what Hinduism strongly recommends for every one of us, whatever may be our station in life. This undercurrent of awareness can be illustrated by a very mundane example, which almost verges on the silly. All of us have memories of our visits to Indian temples. Think of a temple situated in an out-of-the-way location like a village, where there is no organized system of caretaking of your footwear which you leave outside the temple. You go inside the temple, do your prayers, visit the various secondary shrines or *sannadhis* inside the temple, perform *archanas*, wait for the *Archaka* to finish all the formalities of distribution of *prasad* to you, have a look at the architectural beauty of this ancient temple, react to the conversations that comment on the dilapidated way in which they have been keeping these temples, throw away statements like: if only it were America, they would have done it this way and that way, respond to the temple authorities' request for donations for such and such a celebration which is just round the corner,—thus you are engaged in multifarious thoughts and actions. But all the time in your mind there has been an undercurrent of worry about the security of the costly chappals that you have left outside, you have not forgotten where you have kept it, you are trying to speed up matters within the temple so that quickly you may rush to that place and recover it and whatever kind of worship you are doing inside the temple, your subconscious mind is with the chappals. Well, the point is made. That is what one means by an undercurrent of awareness. Now the plea from Hindu religion is only this. In this illustration, God's matters, worship, temple etc. these were all on the outer layers of your mind whereas the inner layer of your consciousness was filled up by the material problem of the safety of the chappals. Can you reverse the status of these two.? While you keep all your material world worries, anxieties and activities,desires and ambitions, plans and strategies, rush and hush, on the outer layers of your mind, can you keep at the bottom portion of your mind, in a *constant, continuous and unbroken way* the awareness that God is present in you and around you and you must thank Him for every moment of your existence? If we can train oneself to make this constant awareness, as part of our system, there is nothing in the world that can overwhelm us, because the strength of the mind now is the strength of the divine. If one has this constant awareness, it will be very difficult for one to stoop to something mean, wrong or corrupt ways of life and behaviour.

It is this attitude of awareness of the divine presence that should be protected for our next generation. In order to sustain it as an unbroken attitude, the *namasankirtana*, the reciting of God's names, is prescribed. And this, namely the practice of *namasankirtana*, is the minimum activity that should be transmitted to the next generation and therefore should be protected and preserved for them, and for their sake, for ourselves. We should not have to resort to long recitations without understanding the meaning. Instead, what we parents and elders want is that our children should imbibe something which would be meaningful to them and which would be of help to their moral and spiritual boosting when the time comes in their life to look for such solace. If today we tell them that the various *stotras* of Hinduism (either in Samskrit or in the regional languages) would bring them intelligence and good ranking in their studies and other activities, and bla-bla-bla, this does not cut any ice with them because the outside world is not in the habit of attaching any values to such things and any way the children think this is only a 'commercial' prayer.

It is suggested therefore that we be satisfied with the essential minimum. Let us not attempt to teach them things which are total mumb-jumbo to them (and perhaps to us also). The children do understand however (we hope!) that there is a God above, and we should pray to Him with a sense of thanksgiving and rememberance. This prayer should be taught to them in such a way that they can catch the meaning without much effort and time. Here comes the aptness of two lines from the *Taittiriyopanishad: tam nama ityupasita, namyante asmai kamah*. This means: If you worship Him with the word '*namah*' then you will have all 'desires' fall at your feet. There is a slight play on the word '*Namah*' in the text here. The word '*namah*' is a very important word in Hinduism. A whole chapter in the *Vedas* is devoted to the repeated use of it with God's names and this chapter called '*Satarudriya*' is considered to be supreme for recitation and repetition in all private and public worship, rituals and ceremonies. The word '*namah*' says not only that you prostrate (before the Lord), but it also says that the prostration indicates '*namama*' or 'nothing is mine', meaning: Everything is Yours, Oh Lord. Desire is the greatest enemy of man and he will never have salvation, according to Hinduism, until he is in control of his desires. The *Upanishad* says that God should be worshipped with the word namah on your lips and in your heart (lips, because of the attitude of prostration, and heart, because of the attitude of surrender of all proprietorship) and this would make all your desires to be at your feet, instead of you falling a prey to your desires. The western way of giving thanks to the Lord is built into and enlarged in Hinduism by the *namaskara* way of paying obeisance to the Lord. Since we want our children to do the minimum possible but at the same time get the maximum benefit when it is time for them to reach out for the divine, the following specific suggestion is made.

Just teach them how to say: *Om Kesavaya namah; Om Narayanaya namah; Om Sivaya namah; Om Durgayai namah; Om Subrahmanyaya namah;* and a few such *namavali*—just a few. Include only those names which mean something to you and which you can explain and have a feeling for. Include such standard names like

Vinayaka or *Ganesa* (because he is the primal God to be worshipped), *Venkatachalapati* (because there is no Hindu who does not belieive in the Lord of Tirupati (and Pittsburgh!) and any other name which connotes your family deity or temple God. For example one may say: *Om Vaideeswaraya namah,* because *Vaideeswara* of Vaideswaran koil may be the family deity. Or one might say *Om Visvanathaya namah,* because the Lord of the Varanasi temple may be needed to be included. Do not include more than fifteen or twenty names. Don't worry about their number. Worry only about the feeling you can generate in the name being worshipped. And most of all, when you expect the child to say these things, ensure that both the parents are also there to say the same thing. Add the *Om* to every such *naamaa* you teach and the word *namah* at the end. *Om* is the symbol of Brahman and so everything starts there and everything ends there. So even if we do not understand anything more of *OM* we should use it. The God's name should be in the dative case; namely, *Kesavaya, Narayanaya, Venkatachalapataye, Lalitayai, Lakshmyai, Saraswatyai,* and so on. At the end have a *Naivedya* to God. Whatever you are going to eat may be offered. And conclude everything with an arti, with or without an arti song or prayer. In this way we would be following the hoary traditions of Hinduism but at the same time we could cut our observances to the coat of our reduced availability of time. By giving this type of discipline instead of the conventional *stotra* recitation, to our children, we would be achieving the following:

> 1. Each child will get a customised instruction, which befits the family and the particular environment and traditions in the family.

2. The child will understand the meaning then and there. We are only paying a homage and obeisance to the particular god named. The different names of god should be justified by appealing to the variety that is always inherent in Hinduism and the fact that the glories of god are innumerable and so therefore their names.

3. The child has infinite varieties of possibilities of expanding this prayer into as long a one as anybody wants, as and when the child is ready for it, because we have only to resort to various *ashtottaras, sahasranamas* and the like—provided there is the motivation and the willingness to spend the time and the effort.

4. By taking care to include *Om* at the beginning of every *naamaa* and '*namah*' at the end of every *naamaa*, we have ensured (hopefully) the help of the Divine in the matter. So even long after we are gone, the 'child' would be ready to spiritually mature —just because of the *Upanishadic* saying.

5. The child does not have to murmur all sorts of mumbo jumbo, which in any case would all vanish into nothingness when we of the previous generation are no more in the scene.

6. The child would have learnt the core of Hindu Bhakti, which is very authentic, and this at almost no cost.

Of course, more fundamental than all this, is the need for ourselves to believe in this, rather than simply make it a preacher's sermon. We should be able to teach by example rather than precept.

CHAPTER 7

Questions and Answers; Problems and Solutions

In the actual presentation of the preceding chapters in the form of lectures to the respective audiences, certain fundamental questions were asked by members of the audience. Some of these questions touch the roots of the Hindu religion and so are important for a global understanding of the Hindu religion particularly for those who reside in a non-Hindu environment. They are therefore discussed below in reasonable detail. The questions which are starred were asked in more than one presentation.

Q. 1. When was God born?

God was not born ever. In fact one of His names is *Ajah*, which means, never born. God is the one unique Truth which is existent in the past, present and future. In fact the Hindu concept of God transcends all time and space. So the question, When was God born, is ill-posed.

But the above answer to this question is rather sophisticated and advanced. The question itself was asked by a ten-year old kid in one of the presentations. It is clear that the question has been asked by the kid, because his parents have told him about *Sri Rama Navami* or *Janmashtami*, referring to the former as Rama's birthday and to the latter as Krishna's birthday. In this context the question is rightly posed, because the kid must have also been told that Rama is God and Krishna is God. At this point it is necessary to bring the con-

cept of Avatar or manifestations of God. (See chapters
1, 2, 3 and 4).

Manifestations of God in concrete form have occurred in every age. The Hindus consider Rama, Krishna,
Jesus and the Buddha among such manifestations.
Whenever *Dharma* declines and *Adharma* is on the rise,
I manifest myself, says the Lord in the Gita. In this sense,
the time of their manifestation is a historical event and
can be called the time of His birth. The birth of Krishna
occurred five thousand and odd years ago. Historians
have yet to confirm this because they do not have in their
hands the evidence of the kind which they usually look
for. Rama's birth, according to the *Ramayana*, occurred
in the *Treta Yuga* of the fifth *Maha Yuga* of the present
Manvantara. Calculation shows that this is 100 million
and odd years ago. It requires faith in the *Ramayana* to
believe this. Nobody seems to have done deep research
into these chronologies with a mind sufficiently open to
bring out more elucidation. See also Answer to Q. 16.

*Q. 2. My mommy says that Jesus and Rama are
both God. How can that be?*
As the question is obviously by a kid, let the answer
be to the kid. Your Mommy is right. In Hinduism, one
of the major principles is that there could be several
paths to God though there is only one God. Each religion is a path to God. We decide which to follow, by
our tradition passed on to us by our ancestors. Hindu
tradition says: There is only one God. He has several
names. Each religion has its own path to God. And
within the same religion, there could be several paths
to God. Again, tradition is the guiding factor here. So
long as the attitudes are right, one does not gain anything by questioning tradition in these matters.

Q. 3. My son goes to school and he comes back learning that Jesus is the only God. But I believe that Hinduism affirms that all religions are true. How do I convince my son that Rama and Krishna are also Gods of worship?

This is actually not a question, but a problem. The solution could be in one of several ways. But whatever may be the method adopted, don't ever intimidate your son. You will never win it. May be you can follow all the suggestions given below.

Suggestion No. 1: Buy the various books by and on Swami Vivekananda, not missing his famous Chicago address. Throw these books at all odd places in the house, to be stumbled upon by your son at all odd times. Do *not* urge him to read the books. Let him stumble upon them wherever he is in the house. One day or other he will read some of them. Wait for as long as one year. Something will happen.

Suggestion No. 2: We shall assume that you have an altar or a place for *Puja* in your residence. Spend a minute to a half hour daily at the altar in total intensity of devotion and prayer. Insist that all the members of your family join you. Show that, along with pictures of Rama and Krishna and other Hindu gods and goddesses, you are not averse to having a picture of Jesus even in your altar. If you have conscientious objections to this, you may have to change your attitude. Otherwise you will not achieve what you want to achieve.

Suggestion No. 3: While you may certainly want to take him to some of the famous Hindu temples in the continent, be not allergic to going to church and praying with the same intensity of devotion. Remember you want to show him that when you say Rama and Krishna are also God, as much as Jesus is, you really mean even more, from your point of view, namely, that Jesus is God as much as Rama and Krishna are to you.

Suggestion No. 4: Back home in India orthodox and tradition-bound people, particularly in the villages have the habit of greeting each other by *Jai Ram ji ki,* and *Ram Ram* (in many parts of North India) and *Narayana* (in some parts of South India). In the western world, having wanted to inculcate 'civilised' habits and manners to your child you must have learnt to say 'God bless you' whenever the child sneezes. Can you learn to say *'Ram Ram'* or *'Narayana'* whenever he sneezes?!

Suggestion No . 5: There is a World Thanksgiving Center in Downtown Dallas, Texas. Take your son there (and, if possible, also the one who taught him that Jesus is the only God) and ask him to talk to people there. World Thanksgiving Center is a movement started to eradicate from this planet the disease of religious intolerance. It is a movement which is being supported by all the great religious leaders of the world, from all religions.

Suggestion No. 6: Talk to the people concerned in the school about the harm they are doing to your son's education as a world citizen. If persuasions fail and if you still feel that in spite of your acting up to the above five suggestions the school is the problem, then pull your son out of that school. The world is wide.

Q. 4. *How do you know that Rama and Krishna are Avatars?*

Listen to the following conversation between an ordinary physics instructor and his student. I = Instructor. S = Student.

S: How do you know, Sir, that Light behaves both as particle and as wave?

J: There is an experiment which is called the two-
    hole experiment, which confirms it and there are
    a few other confirmations.
S: Can I do the two-hold experiment now?
I: No, you would need very expensive equipment
    for doing it. In fact, I myself have never done
    the experiment.
S: Then, Sir, how do you affirm that it is true?
I: I don't have to do the experiment to affirm its
    truth. I know it is an established fact, because
    great scientists have asserted it and many of
    them nobel-laureates. Some of them have cer-
    tainly seen it for themselves by doing the exper-
    iment. Further modern physics concludes a
    number of consequential easily verifiable results
    from this concept of the dual behaviour of light
    and so, even though it is bizarre, it is accepted
    to be true by modern science.

In the same way, I or you do not have to do an
experiment by ourselves to confirm or prove that Rama
or Krishna is an Avatar. There have been great devotees of the Lord,—whose devotion to the Lord is perhaps far greater than the devotion of the greatest
scientists to science—who have affirmed, by their direct
intuition that Rama and Krishna are Avatars. That is
the proof. And here are the names of some of them. Run
through the names, that itself will tell you the weight
of the proof.

The 12 Vaishnava **Alwars** and the 63 Saiva **Nay-
anmars,** spread over the entire first millenium A.D. who
literally 'sang' Hinduism back firmly on the soil of India
in the face of the rise of Buddhism and Jainism, and
whose massive devotional compositions not only broke
the culture away from vedic ritualistic traditions and

piloted it in the direction of Bhakti, but also helped to
make Tamil religious life independent of the knowledge
of Samskrit;

the three great *Acharyas,* **Sankara, Ramanuja and
Madhwa,** who, in a sense are responsible for the fame
of India in religion and philosophy;

the great *Vaishnava Acharyas,* **Pillai Lokacharya,** the
founder of the Tenkalai sect of Vaishnavism and **Vedanta Desikacharya,** the founder of the Vadakalai sect;

Jayadeva, the author of the celebrated *Gita Govinda*
of the 12th century;

Jnaneswar, the Maharashtrian saint-devotee of '*Vit-
thala*' of Pandharpur and the author of an elaborate
commentary of the Gita; his contemporary and asso-
ciate, **Namadeva;**

Bilwamangal, the author of the lilting *Krishna-
karnamrita;*

Swami Ramananda, the apostle of Bhakti in north-
ern India, who changed the face of India from its Vedic
ritualism of the first millenium B.C. to the emotional
Bhakti-centred religion of the 2nd millenium A.D.; his
famous follower, **Kabir,** who was the first exponent and
model of an integration of religions;

Narsi Mehta of Gujarat, **Chandidas** of Bengal, the
Maithili Saint **Vidyapati,** the Karnataka Saint **Puran-
daradasaa** famous for his compositions of *Vitala* and
the founder of Karnatic music, **Talapaka Annama-
charya** the great Telugu *Vaishnava* composer of love
songs on the Lord of Tirumalai, **Surdas** the composer
of *Sur-sagar,*—all of the 15th century;

Sri **Krishna Chaitanya** of Bengal whose life is the
inspiration for the modern Krishna Consciousness
Movement;

Potana, the author of the Telugu *Bhagavatam;*

Tulsidas, the author of *Ramcharitamanas*, who is next only to *Vyasa* and *Valmiki* in the extent of his influence and impact;

Mirabai, the royal devotee of Chittor, **Appayya Dikshidar** of the south, considered by many as an avatar of Sankara himself, **Bhattadri** of Kerala the composer of the well-known *Narayaneeyam* in Samskrit,—all of the 16th century;

The celebrated Marathi saints **Ekanatha**, whose *Bhagavatam* is a literary masterpiece and **Tukaram** the delightful singer of *Abhangas*;

Samarth Ramdas of Maharashtra, the *Guru* of Shivaji, who popularised the thirteen lettered *mantra SRI RAMA JAYA RAMA JAYA JAYA RAMA,* and **Bhakta Ramadas** of Bhadrachalam who built the famous temple out of Government funds and for which it is said that the Lord himself came forward to pay his dues;

Swami **Bodendra Saraswati**, the 59th *Jagadguru* of the *Kamkoti Peetham* and the author of the authoritative work *Namamrita-rasayanam* on the efficacy of the names of God;

The Karnatic musical trinity of Saint-devotees, Sri **Tyagaraja, Shyama Sastri** and **Muthuswami Dikshidar**, all of the 18th century;

Tayumanavar of Tamilnadu and **Ramaprasad** of Bengal;

Bhaskara Raya, the mystic Bhakta of the Goddess and the author of the unique commentary on *Lalita Sahasranama*; and

Ramakrishna Paramahamsa, the gift of Hinduism to posterity; and his own unique gift to posterity, **Swami Vivekananda**, the Messiah.

Q. 5. Does Hinduism admit conversions into it

from members of other religions? Should I (a non-Hindu) become a Hindu?

No. Traditional Hinduism has no set procedures of converting anybody into Hinduism. But, for the past one hundred years, a modern reformist movement which has a large following, called the *Arya Samaj* has streamlined procedures by which a non-Hindu can be converted into Hinduism. Traditional Hinduism has never worried about conversions from another religion into Hinduism because the religion was never missionary in that respect. But there are stories in the history of Hinduism where somebody went over to another religion, and then, was reconverted into Hinduism.

The above is the answer to the question: Could I become a Hindu? But to the question: Should I become a Hindu?, the answer has to be more emphatic. First of all, why should one become a Hindu? What is there so great in Hinduism, which Jesus did not preach or Prophet Mohammed did not propagate.? Hinduism says: If you are a Christian, be a good Christian. By being a good Christian, you are more of a good Hindu than one who has been born in the religion of Hinduism, and does not have the right attitude to other ways of believing in God. Hinduism is a question of attitudes rather than any physical or formal belonging. In fact this is the main reason why Hinduism never cared about conversions into it form other religions.

Q. 6. Would the Hindu religion consider Mahatma Gandhi as an Avatar of God?

No. Mahatma Gandhi was one of the noblest of souls that ever lived on this planet, no doubt. But Avatars of God are of a different category. The word for God in Samskrit is *Bhagavan*. The qualities which characterize one to be called *Bhagavan* include the supernatural capabilities to create and to do miracles by sheer will. In this sense Avatars are different from just noble souls of mankind.

Q. 7. I am told tht a devotee can worship God in any way he likes, provided he has the intensity of devotion. I can offer a flower or a leaf or an animal. If He is going to be happy with any of these, this allows me to give animal sacrifice to my God. What is the stand of Hinduism on this?

There is no question of God being happy or otherwise. Happiness is always in Him. When the Lord says: Offer me a flower or a leaf or water, I shall be pleased, if you offer it with sincerity—it is only a way of saying that this is what you should do. Remember, Krishna is saying this to Arjuna and the conversation there is taking place in the context of two personalities, one a disciple and the other, the teacher. So the words 'pleased' etc. do not imply that God has bouts of happiness and unhappiness.

Coming to the second part of the question about the animal sacrifice, the stand of Hinduism as reflected in the Lord's teaching in the Gita is that it is a question of attitudes and nothing else. Theoretically, 'anything' includes 'animal'. Does this therefore justify animal sacrifice?—this is the implied question by the questioner here. There are stories in the mythological history of India that even meat when offered to the Lord, by a great devotee has been accepted by the Lord—in the sense that the devotee's devotion has been blessed and in fact became a model for the rest of humanity. We are referring to the story of Kannappa Nayanar here. But what was the attitude of Kannappa Nayanar in that?

He was ready to pluck his remaining eye for the sake of donating it to the Lord, even though he was already blind by one eye which he had just plucked and offered to Him! In such a case of extreme devotion, the attitude was obvious and the blessing of the Lord was automatic.

It is also true that in Vedic times there were animal sacrifices and these were part of certain rituals, which had been in vogue almost till recent times. But it was merely because of the misuse of these that a Buddha had to appear on the scene and wean people away from their other-worldly ambitions and make them concentrate on compassion, sympathy and non-violence as one's basic *dharmas*. It was because of the misdirected emphasis on the ritualistic sacrifices still persisting even after the Buddha's time, that a Sankara appeared and emphasised the transience of every benefit whether of this world or of the other world and led everybody on to think in terms of their upward path of evolution rather than keep circling in the quagmire of the cycle of births and deaths.

If we are going to do animal sacrifice for the Lord,in the hope of eating that *Prasad* and gratifying our senses or in the hope of getting something from the Lord in terms of a benefit, material or otherwise, this attitude of selfishness will certainly be known to the Lord, who is in our heart of hearts and He is not going to accept it as a token of Bhakti. (See the chapter 5, in entirety). In all cases of a dilemma of *Dharma*, the stand of Hinduism is clear, whatever may be said by the secondary scriptures. Any time when there is even an iota of selfishness or self-aggrandisement in what we do, it is against *dharma*.

Q. 8. How did mind, which is material, attach itself to something that is divine, namely the soul? And when did it do so?

The question implies that the mind was unattached to the soul originally and then at some point of time became attached to the soul. If we rightly understand the concept of mind in Hindu metaphysics, we would discover that there is nothing like mind on its own. It is only a flow of thoughts on the subtle bed of *vasanas*. It is only a bundle of desires. If there were no thoughts or desires there is no mind. The mind is like a pile of bricks; the moment the bricks vanish there is no pile. The very existence of mind as an entity implies that there is a past, from which the *vasanas* have been inherited and these are the ones which stick to the soul in the form of the mind. If there was no past, there is no *vasana*, no mind. Hindu metaphysics proceeds on the assumption that there is an eternal past the beginning of which is non-existent. Even in the so-called *pralaya* time, when everything in the universe merge into *Brahma* the creator, the *vasanas* are existent in a latent form attached to individual souls. It is these that blossom in the next (cosmic) day of *Brahma*. Thus the question whether mind did attach itself to the individual soul at a specific point of time does not arise. (see chapters 1, 2, & 6).

Q. 9. Christianity says that man is born a sinner. Hinduism says, according to you, that man is divine. How do you reconcile this and still maintain that all religions are true?

Hinduism says that man is essentially divine. In other words if you peel off all the external matter in man, including his mind and its makings, the entity that is left is the individual soul and this is divine. This *Jivatma*, as it is called, is nothing but a fragment of the infinite transcendental *Para Brahman*, the only Ultimate Reality ever. So what is sinning is the mind, which brings in the ego and though it carries on all its drama and gets its life from the individual soul with which it is attached. The very existence of the mind is because of the past *vasanas*. In this sense mind is the sinner. Thus, talking in the language of the Christian viewpoint, we must say that man, with the sense of ego in him is the sinner; but man by himself, namely, the individual soul, rid of all the ego in him and therefore rid of the mind, is divine.

Q. 10. *Why does Hinduism extol the action of Rama in implicitly obeying his father and step-mother to go to the forest? How do we tell this to modern children who are not able to appreciate the logic behind this?*
The entire scriptural literature with all its *Puranas*, legends and stories are one on this point that a father's word is law for the son. In ancient times this was so much of a truism that nobody even wanted a justification for this. Indeed when *Bh rata* and all his elders and courtiers went to *Chitrakuta* to bring back Rama to Ayodhya, and there was a long plea by *Bharata* to Rama that the latter should simply come back, because everyone wants him back and *Bharata* would even substitute for him in the forest, Rama begins by saying only one sentence which seals the conversation for the day, even though all the great ministers and rishis were present there. This one sentence is a half verse in *Valmiki's Ramayana* and runs thus:

Mata pitrubhyamuktoham katham anyat samachare?

This means: When I have been told so by my

mother and father, how can I do otherwise? Nobody had any reply to this powerful statement. They all dispersed for that day. The conversation resumed the next morning with *Bharata* opening up new angles of argument. Well, the story goes on.

For our purposes we should only note here how electrical the effect of that single statement was on that august assemblage of scholars, elders and experts. In order to tell our present day kids why every one in the Hindu cultural milieu considers this obedience to father and mother as so important, let me quote below from *Manu Smriti* the relevant portion which stipulates and justifies this universal requirement of Hindu *Dharma*. If there is anything in Hindu scriptures which may be considered to be as powerful and as emphatic and precise as The Ten Commandments of Christendom, it is this portion of the *Manu Smriti*. We just quote seven *slokas*:

> *yam mata pitarau klesam sahete sambhave nrinam na tasya nishkritihsakya kartum varsha-satairapi.*

> *tayor-nityam priyam kuryat acharyasya cha sarvada teshveva trishu tushteshu tapah sarvam samapyate.*

> *tesham trayanam susrusha paramam tapa uchyate na tair-abhyananujnato dharmam-anyam samacharet.*

> *ta eva hi trayo lokah ta eva traya asramah ta eva hi trayo vedah ta evoktas-trayognayah.*

> *pita vai garhapatyognihmataagnir-dakshinah smritah guru-rahavaniyas-tu sagni-treta gariyasi.*

yavat-trayas-te jiveyuh tavan-nanyam
samacharet teshveva nityam sushrusham
kuryat priyahite ratah.

trishveteshviti krityam hi purushasya samap-
yate esha dharmah paras-sakshat upa-
dharmo-nya uchyate.

Meaning, that there is nothing in the three worlds which can compensate for the pains and sufferings that the parents, mother and father, have gone through in bringing up the son both at the time of birth and after. Even in one hundred years one cannot repay the debt which one owes to them. To the two of them and to the *Guru*, one should always do what is pleasing to them. If these three are satisfied, all *dharma*, penances and obligations stand fulfilled. The service to these three is the summum bonum of all penances. Without their permission no other *dharma* should be observed. They are the three worlds (*Bhur, Bhuvah, Suvah*), they are the three *asramas* (*brahmacharya, grihasta and vanaprastha*), they are the three *vedas* (*Rig, Yajur, Sama*), and they are the three sacred Fires of the Vedic tradition. The father is the *Garhapatya* Fire, the mother is the *Dakshina* Fire, the *guru* is the *Ahavaniya* Fire. This Trinity of the three Fires is most sacred. As long as those three are living one should not have to observe any other dharma or penance. Anyone who is interested in his well being should serve daily these three most sincerely. A man's entire obligation for life is fulfilled if these three are taken care of. This is the suprememost *dharma*. Everything else is only a secondary *dharma*.

Q. 11. Why should we accept that there is a God?
Accepting God is purely a subjective experience.

It has nothing to do with the logic and the rationale of the external world, though there have been very sincere attempts made by great minds all over the world and all through the centuries, to rationalise the existence of God. According to Hinduism one has to take it on faith form the scriptures and from the postulation by the elders and then *go on to discover it for oneself, by oneself, in oneself.* The greatness of Hinduism rests on the fact that this has been done by thousands of people even in the small historical portion of the past.

*Q. 12. Should we believe in Advaita or Dvaita?
*Q. 13. If the great teachers like Sankara, Ramanuja and others differ in their interpretations of the scriptures, which of them do we follow? Is there a possibility of integration of all these interpretations?

These two questions, in some form or other, have been asked at almost every presentation. Let us answer them together, since the subject-matter of the questions is the same. Sankara and Ramanuja the two great founders of the two major schools of philosophy of Hindu India differ only in one point. In interpreting the *Upanishads*, to which of the statements shall we give importance or dominance? To the statements that are obviously absolutist? Or to those that are obviously non-absolutist? Sankara supports the former viewpoint and Ramanuja leans towards the latter. This difference in interpretation by these two great teachers has generated a succession of philosophical literature by later thinkers and writers and the body of literature on both sides is voluminous. For us ordinary seekers of God, the difference between Sankara and Ramanuja should not matter. For, said in technical terms, Sankara says there is ultimately no distinction between God, souls

and matter because souls and matter are nothing but
divine, though in the phenomenal world they appear
to be different. Ramanuja says that the phenomenal difference persists in the ultimate also though in a subtle
way. Now for us in the phenomenal world, what does
it matter whether this phenomenal difference persists
in the ultimate or not? Let us cross the bridge when we
come to it. As far as the phenomenal world is concerned,
both Sankara and Ramanuja and all the other Masters
of the other schools of philosophy agree that we have
to purify our minds through Bhakti, we have to eradicate all our undesirable *vasanas* in the first instance, we
have to surrender even our will to God and work in
this world in a totally unselfish manner. Thus the teaching of the great masters coincide in terms of what we
have to do in the real world. In fact this is why Hindu
religion is one in spite of all the differences in interpretations of the scriptures. Summarising from the
introductory analysis in the chapter on *Jnana* in the book
'Essentials of Hinduism' we may say that Reality is probably multidimensional, but our phenomenal world and
our minds are one-dimensional and though the different Masters differ in their descriptions of the multidimensional reality the one-dimensional projection from
any of their descriptions happens to be the same and
this is what matters to us.

Let us follow therefore the One Master whom our
ancestors have followed. To try to adjudicate between
the two either on the academic plane or on the ritualistic plane will be more than a life time task and it
is not worth it. To try to integrate the two viewpoints
on the academic plane will be well-nigh impossible
because if that were possible the two Masters themselves would have done it. The sage Ramakrishna has,

with his characteristic authenticity on such matters, given the verdict that it is a question of your own evolution and taste and that we should not attempt to discard one in favour of the other. As far as our daily chores are concerned follow the teachings of both and as far as the logic on the intellectual plane is concerned follow the One Master who is your Master by your tradition and ancestry, for otherwise you will get lost like the grammarian whose grammar could not save him while he was sinking.

Q. 14. Maybe, as you say, there was no religious intolerance by the Hindus of other religions. But within the religion of Hinduism itself, how do you explain the continuous war, verging on political violence, that was waged between Saivites and Vaishnavites, for centuries, particularly in South India?

Arrogance at an intellectual level, political scheming, royal affluence, passionate devotion to one particular manifestation of God and a culture that prevailed in those times wherein victory in an intellectual argumentative debate would win you even royal favour— the compounding effect of all these resulted in those battles for religious supremacy. The intellectual arrogance that arises out of a capability to do academic dialectics, which assumes for itself the correctness of all its interpretations, of the same scriptures which both parties swear to, is a valid disease even in modern times. The only antidote which will compensate for and eradicate this arrogance is humility that arises out of bhakti to the Lord, and the humility that is characteristic of the quest confronted by a heritage several thousands of years old. This also explains why Questions 12 and 13 have been answered the way they have been.

Q. 15. The daily practice of Hinduism allows and sustains prayers to God, particularly to the deities enshrined in the temples, of a commercial kind; for example, Oh God, if such and such a good thing happens to me I will come to your temple and offer worship, and so on. Is not this practice questionable? How do you justify this?

There are two kinds of such prayers. One kind is when you go and offer what you want to offer to the deity and then pray that you should achieve the ambition in your mind. But the other kind is more commercial. It would not offer the offering to the deity until the object of the desire is fulfilled. This second kind is the one which is practised more often. In the case of the first kind at least your trust in God has some credibility. In the case of the second there is no difference between this deal with God and the deal with a partner in business. Perhaps in reality one trusts the business partner more than one trusts God.

It is only religious and spiritual evolution that can change these habits. But look at it from God's point of view, if there be one such. He created you, me and all and is waiting there for you to come back to Him and ask Him for what He is always ready to give, namely the ultimate salvation. Instead, we go to Him and ask for all the petty things of the world. And the irony and agony of God is He keeps on giving all the things you want so that ultimately you may want what He wants to give you.!

Q. 16. You said that Krishnavatara happened five thousand and odd years ago. But historians have a different perception of these chronologies. How do you reconcile the mystical chronology advocated by the orthodox Hindu religion and scientific concepts of chronology of events?

Historians will keep changing their perception when more and more evidence falls into their hands. This is a dynamic process. But the past is a single static fact. In order to understand it right we have to do more research. In trying to do this kind of research, in addition to relying on all the archeological and historical evidence in the scientific way, we should be able to do literary search and research into the innumerable mythological literature, temple *Sthala Puranas,* and so on, keeping an open mind. Until this kind of research leads to specific results, we cannot expect to have a categorical answer to this question.

Q. 17. What is wrong in meat-eating? Why does Hinduism extol vegetarianism?

According to the central teaching contained in the myriad scriptures of Hinduism, everything that is animate is but a spark of the omnipresent Divinity. Therefore no harm should be done to anything that is living. This is the principle of non-violence which is one of the basic virtues recommended for the upward path of evolution of the soul. But like any other virtue, like Truth for example, it is an expression of an ideal state only. The more one toils to reach that perfection the nearer one is to the goal on the upward path.

In fact eating plant food is also a kind of harm done to the plant world. Here comes a delicate balance. Earth is the most concrete form of expression of Nature through its five elements. These five elements themselves—earth, water, fire, air and space—are nothing but expressions of the same Divinity. This expression is what is technically known as *Prakriti.* So for worship, we take the most concrete form of *Prakriti* and that is why, the *Linga* and the *Saalagrama* made of earth are worshipped as the forms bordering the form- less. Plants are the next in evolution from this concrete form of *Prakriti*. But still they have no soul. Animals have a soul. So they should not be killed. Eating plant food with proper discipline is called vegetarianism.

Q. 18. I am a soldier fighting a war which I think is totally unjustifiable. What does Hinduism have to say on a dilemma like this?

The entire *Bhagavad-Gita* is the answer to this ques- tion. It is not to be expected that one can condense the contents of the Gita here. Still, to be brief,one might say that this kind of dilemma does not only occur on the battlefields but it occurs in one's daily life, in the office, in one's relations with his contemporaries, in fact everywhere. The Gita says: Act with detachment in an unselfish manner; take things in their stride; have faith in God; do your duty irrespective of their consequen- ces; if things are not in your control, take it as God's will; have no desires for yourself, even in respect of the justness or otherwise of your action; whether you will die in the war or not, whether you will succeed in your enterprise or not, leave the decision to God; and act in the living present.

*Q. 19. Why do devotees suffer?

The elementary answer is that God tests them to gauge the intensity of their belief and devotion. This answer is indeed given by many exponents of Hindu- ism and is also mentioned in some contexts in the *Pura- nas*. But experts in the scriptures do not accept this answer. It was in one of Sri Krishna Premi's lectures that I gathered the right answer to this question. The elementary answer only underestimates the omniscience of God. He has no necessity to test us, ordinary mortals. He clearly knows that we will fail in such tests. But then this theory of God testing His devotees is certainly true in the case of confirmed intense devotees of the Lord. In such cases, He tests them just to show to the rest of the world how intense and effective is their devotion and how far a devotee's faith can carry him. He knows that they won't fail His test. In our ordinary cases, the theory that God tests us is not acceptable. We suffer because of our Karma. And we have to suffer it. Hinduism is very clear on this point. In fact even in the case of leading devotees they could not avoid the suffering that they had to endure. But their lives show how when the Lord's Grace descended on them, the most intense suffering could be either transformed into intense delight or, more often than not, God's Grace, instead of wiping out their suffering provided an insulation of faith which enabled them to be oblivious of that suffering underneath.

Q. 20. What is the meaning of Namaste?

Namaste is a Samskrit compound word made up of two words *namah* and *te*. *Te* means to *you* .. *Namah* means *salutations* or *prostrations*. So the simple meaning is: salutations to you.This seems to be quite an innocuous statement. But there is a deeper meaning. When I say '*namaste*' to you the words 'to you' certainly refer to the physical 'you' standing or sitting before me but they in fact refer to the Divinity inside you. Otherwise the word '*namah*' which indicates extraordinary respect would not be compatible when addressed to equals. The word *namah* is used in making prostrations

to God and is the repetitively used word when we worship God in the *archana* form, saying for example, *Om
Kesavaya namah, Om Narayanaya namah* and so on. In
each such case the *namah* is not simple prostration. The
namaskara that is implied in the word *namah* indicates,
according to Sri Sathya Sai Baba, an attitude of *na-mama-
kara* that is, the attitude of 'not mine'. In other words
when you make a prostration to the Lord saying *namah*,
you assume an attitude of total surrender to the Lord,
saying that everything I have is yours, Oh Lord; nothing
is mine. The *Upanishads* say therefore that if you worship God with this attitude of surrender expressed
through the words *namah*, then all desires will prostrate
at your feet—meaning, you will ultimately conquer all
desires. The word *namah* has such a deep meaning and
so when this word is used to greet the person opposite
it is not simply an equivalent of a secular greeting used
in our everyday world. It is actually a recognition of the
divinity within the person opposite you and it is to that
divinity that you are prostrating with an attitude of surrender, that is, an attitude of *na-mama-kara* in the awareness of the presence of the ever-present Divinity.

*Q. 21. You seem to be emphasizing the importance
of attitudes as against rituals. But don't you see that
these attitudes will themselves become rituals in due
course of time?*

This is a theoretical impossibility. For, attitude is
a frame of mind and a frame of mind can never become
a ritual. A ritual is an action which is done without putting your mind and heart in it, almost mechanically and
very often without your having any faith in the purpose for which it is done or supposed to be done. The
right attitudes to a religious ritual come from the under-

standing of either the contextual or the esoteric meanings of the procedures and the chantings which constitute the ritual. This is too much to ask from an average person. So the correct frame of mind has to be developed by agreeing that rituals have a meaning in one or more of the following situations, and I quote from the book 'Essentials of Hinduism', p. 21: "(1) when one is young or spiritually immature and has to learn self-discipline; (ii) when one is tuned up to it spiritually and the rituals are a bubbling forth of one's internal convictios; (iii) when one is too much of the world—for such a person rituals are the reins by which he controls, though for a brief spell only, the running away of his sense-horses, carried away by kama, krodha, lobha, etc.; and (iv) when one is mature enough to understand that rituals are a means to an end and not the end itself." The correct frame of mind may in turn become a habit and this is what exactly we want.

Q. 22. By saying that the Ultimate Supreme is the only Reality and by saying that everything else is transient and therefore not important, is not Hinduism underrating the importance of daily worldly life and is this not the reason why India is behind many other nations in material prosperity inspite of its massive manpower resource?"

Ultimate Supreme is the only Reality, Yes. Everything else is transient—Yes. But the next statement is wrong. Hinduism does not say therefore the worldly life is not important. If they had said it is not important, the context means that they are not important for the ultimate objective of life, namely *moksha*.. But there are three other objectives of life, namely, *dharma, artha* and *kama*. The pursuit of *artha*—meaning material wealth and prosperity—or the pursuit of *kama*—

meaning all desires, including those that are sensual —, are both legitimate objectives of life, *provided* they are pursued in concordance with the first objective, namely *dharma*. The pursuit of *artha* and *kama* in a way acceptable to *dharma* simply means that *artha* and *kama* should be pursued as per the scriptural injunctions in terms of self-discipline and societal discipline. The daily worldly life is considered to be so important in Hinduism that they have cared to lay down, in full elaboration and micro-detail, rules and injunctions starting from the morning ablutions and going all the way through the day upto the time that you go to bed. They invade even the privacy of your bedroom and lay down several do's and don'ts. These scriptural injunctions are there just to inculcate into you habits which you will never have to unlearn even when the time comes for you to look for something beyond the three objectives of dharma, artha and kama.

It is a familiar sight in some American campuses of universities just before Christmas time to see some such sign board: 'Drive carefully. ONE IN TWENTY AMONG YOU WOULD NOT RETURN AFTER CHRISTMAS. DO YOU WANT TO BE THAT ONE?" Shall we say that this dampens Christmas vacation enjoyment or that it considers Christmas vacation unimportant.? It only urges you to have an undercurrent of carefulness even as you enjoy your vacation, driving. So also, Hinduism, with that paternalistic concern that it exhibits for your ultimate welfare, in all its scriptures, makes it clear to you in no unmistakable terms that your enjoyment of the driving and piloting of this real worldly life is not that important for you to exceed your speed limits, if you really have any ambition to look beyond!. The father of saintliness in the

Tamil world said this most succinctly almost two thousand years ago: Do all the good you can before the last hiccup deactivates your tongue. (*naacherru vikkul mel vaaraamun nalvinai merchenru cheyyappadum*).

The modern scientists—some of them—make the mistake of thinking that they would find the truth of everything without first knowing themselves alright. But Hindu religion is clear that the more important thing is to know oneself right. How else do you prevent the misuse of science for war and terrorism? In the western world, philosophy and philosophical ideas are sometimes equated with exercises in futility, just because, philosophy was studied by looking for evidence for the validity of its ideas from everyday common experience of man and from the experience of his sense perception. How can this lead to the truth, when one has not recognised the primary ignorance about the divinity of man.? Even the usefulness of intellect is limited because intellect itself starts with a primary ignorance about man's innate divinity.

Q. 23. Can women recite ritualistic prayers like the vedas and special mantras, which are denied to them by orthodox opinion?

In one of the *Upanishads*, right in the middle, there is a passage which is preceded by the words: At this point let pregnant women move away from here; and followed by the words: At this point let pregnant women come back. This shows that women were, as a rule, part of whatever was being recited or discussed in those *Upanishadic* times. There are several other examples. So there is no reason why women cannot learn the *vedas* or the *mantras*. At the same time the rule that no *mantra* can be efficacious unless it is learnt orally

from a *guru*, who has himself that *mantra-siddhi* has also
to respected. By *mantra-siddhi*, one means that the *mantra*
has sufficiently been meditated upon and repeated by
the person concerned that the deity of the *mantra* has
been realised by the person. The word *mantra* in Samskrit means that which protects by being meditated upon.
Mananat trayate iti mantrah.. This protection by the *devata*
of the *mantra*, does not devolve on you until you have
sufficiently identified yourself with the *mantra*, heart
and soul. Only such a person can be a *guru* for that
mantra. So those of us who want to learn a *mantra*, for
purposes of meditation or *japa* or what-have-you, must
have the patience to look for the right *guru* of that particular *mantra*. When such a *guru* is available, certainly
one can go ahead.

Q. 24. How do we explain the caste system?
See the book 'Essentials of Hinduism' for an academic explanation. If however the question is the outcome of a doubt as to how we are to justify the caste
system to the next generation, it is to be said that there
is no such need. For, there is no caste system for the
next generation. For instance, where is the brahmin in
modern times.? If you follow the caste system and the
scriptures which talk about it, a brahmin ceases to be
a brahmin the moment he does one of the following:
(this is not an exhaustive list!) (i) defaults on his *Gayatri Japa*; (ii) sells his knowledge; (ii) accepts a bribe; (iv)
urinates, like an animal, while standing; or (v) copu-
lates without wanting a progeny. In these circumstances, no explanation of the ancient caste system is
relevant except on an academic plane, to understand
the past. The only words of relevance are the ones which
occur in the Gita where the Lord talks about the cor-

rect attitude of a man of wisdom. These are the lines which Mahatma Gandhi used to like very much and would listen to their recitation often. He was more of a brahmin than all the brahmins by birth. A brahmin by attitude is what every world citizen should strive for. In the country which gave the world the greatest apostle of non-violence, we must not have any doubts about Truth and Non-violence being more basic social virtues than a social system like the caste system. Any action or thought which implies even an iota of self-ishness or self-aggrandisement is Adharma and this fundamental principle vetoes any such so-called 'dhar-mic' action done in the name of caste. The moment one member of one caste feels violently hurt when another caste considers him either under-privileged or over-privileged because of his birth in a so-called caste, the moment one caste assumes an arrogant attitude and considers members of another caste either under-equipped or over-equipped because of their birth, the principles of non-violence apply and the rules of the caste system are no more justifiable. On the other hand, individual obligations, like purity, self-control and detachment, which do not have anything to do with the other man, must be preserved and followed. However, one who has been initiated, into the *Gayatri Japa*, for example, has the added responsibility of practising it regularly and preserving it, because, that is the mini-mum price he pays for having had access to the most sacred of all *mantras* of Hinduism.

Q. 25. If everything happens by the Will of God, does it mean that we don't have any free will and cannot achieve anything by ourselves?

Man does have a free will. He has the free will to

do things he is not supposed to do. He has the free will to become an alcoholic and be a nuisance to society. He has also the free will to be gentle, compassionate, sympathetic and helpful. He has the free will to choose his path. This is one of the fundamental assumptions of not only Hinduism, but of all religions as well. For if that were not so, where is the need for the commandments of God and for rules that scriptures lay down for man's conduct? The very idea of a commandment and an injunction like: Speak the truth, implies that you have the free will to obey or to disobey. You may have the will to disobey, but religion says: *have the willingness to obey*. Of your own free will decide to follow scriptures and come to God. That is why, in Hinduism, God waits until you have shown at least an iota of interest in Him. When we say that everything happens according to the Will of god, we specifically refer to Nature and Nature's doings. When an event happens to a human or a living being (with a soul) and this is referred to as God's Will, this is only a way of saying that it is one's past Karma that has brought about this event. Note carefully the average Hindu psychology here. When a bad thing happens to somebody it is said that is God's Will. But when a good thing happens to us, we don't say that it is God's Will. The teaching of religion is: Either learn to accept both as God's Will or, in the alternative, learn to take responsibility for both. Don't blame only the unpleasant things on God. When Hinduism constantly repeats that everything is God's Will, it is to teach you a certain humility and to prevent you from being bloated by arrogance into thinking that *you* achieved what you achieved.

*Q. 26. How do we (Hindu non-residents) moti-

*vate the next generation to learn about the Hindu way
of life and believe in it?*

This whole book is the answer to this question.
However, if a brief answer is required, here is one. The
only way seems to be by ourselves living the Hindu
way of life and believing in it. Without any effort to correct our own individual behaviour not only in temples
and during special functions, but in terms of our daily
life all the 24 hours, we cannot hope to transmit to the
next generation any Hindu values of life by sheer word
of mouth. If there is an altar in the house, let us discipline ourselves to spend a few minutes (preferably
half an hour) daily—every day at the same time—for
both a silent meditation and a recitation of God's names
as was suggested in Chapter 6. It is important that all
the members of the family be present together at this
time of prayer. One should not hesitate on this score
that back home in India we did not do such things. In
the Christian world there is a commendable practice
that when you sit together for meal you thank the Lord
and pray together, at the beginning of the meal. The
Hindu substitute for this could be a common prayer at
the altar either in the morning before we go to work
or in the evening time before all sit for dinner. This
channelisation in cultural habits is a must if we want
our children to imbibe something from the Hindu culture. Any effort on our part to teach something which
we do not ourselves do or understand will not be pro-
ductive. It will actually be counter-productive.

*Q. 27. You have said, many times that it is the
attitudes that are important rather than a physical
expression of the ritual or the action. What is your
authority for saying this.?*

If scriptures are to be quoted it can be done. Every verse from the Gita where it talks about renunciation or detachment or bhakti, mentions it is the mental attitude of renunciation or detachment or bhakti or surrender that is important rather than the physical action. The more one delves deep into Hinduism one discovers that it is all a question of attitudes only. But my own conviction stems from the fact that I have observed quite closely certain persons of the previous generation who taught me more by example than by precept in this context. My father was one of them. I have seen how much of a *stitha-prajnata (meaning, firmness of wisdom*—talked about in the Gita) this kind of behaviour can generate in oneself. That is my authority.

Om Santih Santih Santih.

Reference.

V. Krishnamurthy: Essentials of Hinduism. Narosa Publishing House, New Delhi. (1989)